# Living with Anxiety and Depression

by

HERBERT H. KRAUSS
BEATRICE JOY KRAUSS

THOMAS
MORE
PRESS

ISBN: 0-88347-035-7

# Contents

# Acknowledgments

We would like to acknowledge, in print, our debt to the following individuals who have helped us with this book: Mrs. Mable Osgood, Ms. Patricia McNally, and Mr. Richard Rogoski. Their aid has proved invaluable.

# Preface

This is a small book. Its intent is to provide the general reader with information about the nature of anxiety and depression. To accomplish this, the book ranges from such topics as how anxiety and depression feel to how to cope with those feelings. Because this is a little book, it cannot be a "how to" book. In fact, no book, whatever its length, could adequately fulfill that purpose. In spite of that inadequacy, we hope this book may help some people deal with their problems in a more adequate fashion.

The reader also should be aware that this book is somewhat biased. Social aspects of anxiety and depression are emphasized. Little information has been provided about the physiology of anxiety and depression, or the medical treatment of such conditions. Please bear that in mind. This is especially important to remember if you intend to use this book to aid you when you are worried and feeling miserable. If you feel bad and have for some time, the first step you should take is to schedule a complete medical checkup, not read this book.

# CHAPTER ONE

# The Experience of Depression and Anxiety

The small and large crises of life are understood best from the inside. Often we find ourselves turning for leadership to those who have felt life weigh in on them and, like a green stick passed through fire, have emerged strengthened by the experience. Abraham Lincoln, for example, faced the bloodbath of the Civil War with a determination that Carl Sandburg felt was born of Lincoln's own personal suffering, the loss of his two sons and his continual struggle with periods of depression and anxiety during which he questioned his goals and his leadership and the terrible price the country was paying for them. It was said that before signing the Emancipation Proclamation, Lincoln's hand shook so violently in his anxiety that he discarded a number of pens before he found the ability to sign the document firmly.

All of us have experienced depressions and anxieties, in more or less severe forms, as life presents us with problems which we meet initially with withdrawal or fear. For each age, each thread of individual life may bring different problems of differing severity. Often, the external circumstances of a crisis may belie the internal agony of the individual encountering it. For example, going to a funeral may be a solemn task for an older woman resigned to the experience of seeing her friends and relatives diminish in number. Going to the same funeral may precipitate a confusion and panic terrible to bear in a young woman who recently lost a young child and does not know if she was negligent as a mother. In each of the cases of anxiety and depression reported below, the reader should keep in mind how the external circumstances affect the internal needs of the individual. The reader should also keep in mind that the psychological experiences of anxiety and depression are inevitably accompanied by bodily reactions which, in themselves, often become another crisis to weather. Each case history is a factual one, although the names of the people involved have been changed.

## Depressive Reaction to Bereavement

It has been 3 months almost to the day since Mr. S. had died. Mrs. S. turned in her bed to look at the clock. 10:14 a.m. She knew it was a crime to stay in bed so late, but then, what did she have to get up for? No one needed her. The children were grown and had families of their own, and Mr. S. was gone. She wasn't hungry, not hungry enough to get up and make breakfast. She looked with indifference at the thick layer of dust which lay upon the furniture of the small apartment. The apple core rotting on the dresser, the unopened mail, the general disorder of the apartment did not offend her as it would have a year ago. She felt as if her life was gone, sucked out of her in the awful nights when she knew her life-long companion was dying. "I gave and gave," she thought, "and now I am gone. This is what they must mean by 'spent.'" Her eyes rested momentarily on the lamp on the bedside table. Tears and then sobs broke from her, as the lamp which had stood beside the bed in 3 houses through 26 long years, which Mr. S. had turned out each night as his last household duty, evoked a torrent of emotions and memories. "I was good to him; I wronged him; he needed me; I am useless." These and many other thoughts poured through her mind. Mrs. S. had given so much to him and had gotten so much in return that it was impossible to conceive of loving again, of opening herself to someone and then to feel again the terrible pain she felt now. Perhaps it was better to die. In her pain and sorrow, in her bereavement, it was hard to see into the next year. The love she had invested in her husband would slowly turn toward her neighbors, children, and grandchildren. The lassitude and tiredness would lighten and she would be baking pies and visiting again. That her children should ever

**11**

remark about her courage was as far from her heart at that moment as the morning sun shining through the dirty windows of her lonely apartment.

### Anxiety and Depression in Reaction to Failure

Rich's first reaction had been anger. "Who the hell are they to fail me? A stinking, dirty, little southern university with no national reputation to speak of. I went to *Yale* as an undergrad," etc., etc. His second reaction was self-doubt that wore at his feelings of worth through the following days. Why didn't he have a girl friend? Was he incapable of love? Could this show in his exam papers? Did they know who he really was? If he couldn't pass the exam, what could he do? He had always wanted to be a doctor; he had never thought of anything else. He had been arrested last week for a traffic violation and the policeman had talked to him coldly. He had been humiliated and he didn't fight back. He had called to tell his father about the exam and to ask for money to cover the fine. His parents had been indifferent, too. He became frightened; his world was coming apart, flying away in all directions. He paced aimlessly; he couldn't study. He wasn't a doctor, he wasn't a son, he wasn't anyone's boyfriend, he wasn't even a man. Then it came to him in a flash: he would be nobody. He went to a party that night, drank a lot, stayed aloof. They were surprised, but not shocked, when they found him hanging from a railing, his necktie in a noose around his neck.

## Depressive Reaction to Surgery

Mr. T. awoke in his hospital bed. It took him a few minutes to shake off the anesthesia and realize where he was and why he was there. So the operation, a minor one, had gone smoothly. He was overcome with a sense of relief, a feeling of well-being and a zest for life. That day he joked with his visitors, teased the nurses, grew sentimental over the flowers, and told the office he'd be back next week. He told the doctors he had never felt better and they told him the adrenalin was just pumping through his body in reaction to the operation and please would he prepare himself for a letdown.

With great plans for catching up on the work he'd missed, Mr. T. set out for work on Monday. By noon, Mr. T.'s mood had done an about-face. He just couldn't bring it off. He was tired, frustrated at being tired, angry and depressed. He went home to sleep and to brood about all those things that everyone broods about when faced by illness or operations: death, personal competence, the personal resources needed to deal with bodily injury (money, help of family, friends, understanding of those at work). Mr. T., so used to being an organizer, a mover, a doer, was suffering a loss

**13**

of faith in himself and his abilities. There was much less energy available to his body, but he was still making his usual demands on it. Mr. T. felt frail, frightened and sad. Was the sleepy man in the bed he? Was he going to be like this the rest of his life? The answer, of course, was no. What Mr. T. needed was a little more time to heal, a little patience, and a temporary reorganization of the standards he set for himself.

## Depression Accompanying Decisions

The hardest thing about choosing, thought Joe, was that making a choice meant that all other alternatives were forsaken. There was one life to live and this was it. He sat with his head in his hands. He should be happy, he thought. Both alternatives were good ones. He could accept the offer from the small electronics firm in the Pacific Northwest. His salary would not be large, but he could see his two boys growing up by the green mountains and fishing with him in the cool, blue lakes. Or he could accept the offer from the large industry in the Eastern city. The salary was very good; his wife would be near friends and relatives, but they would have to live in an apartment or commute. It hinged on these questions: What kind of people are we? What is important to the family? They would be leaving behind the friends they had made here, and he wondered if they would ever be this happy again.

Joe's sense of loss warred with his expectations for the future. The future was uncertain, but the loss was sure. The happy decision definitely had its dark side.

In all of the cases noted above, a sense of loss is present—loss of a loved one, loss of identity, loss of abilities, loss of a lifestyle. In the studies of anxiety, a central theme is fear, a fear in which the outcome, and sometimes the object, of the fear is unknown. Many times anxiety and depression occur together, for often life presents us with a fear that a loss may occur.

## An Anxiety Attack

Joan had been 24 years old and 3 months into her third pregnancy when her second son had died. A smiling toddler of 18 months, he had suddenly spiked a fever and gone into convulsions. The next day he was dead of spinal meningitis. Soon her third child was due. In so many ways she was grateful for the life within her. If only this time nothing would go wrong.

An uncle had died and Joan went to his funeral. Relatives and friends looked at her solicitously when she arrived. She had seen their look of sympathy before. Like a shock wave, panic broke through her body. They had looked at her the same way at her baby's funeral. It was wrong, illogical. How could she do this to her aunt? She was screaming, "Don't look at me. It won't happen. It will never happen again." She was

**15**

hysterical with fear and was fighting against her husband who was pulling her from the church. She was dimly aware that it was wrong of her to behave this way. Her poor aunt.

Every part of her body wanted to run, to scream, to fight, to kick, to protect her from the dark possibility shoved once more before her face. Her sister came running to her side and gently led her from the church. They walked together until fatigue caused the panic to subside. Joan had experienced an anxiety attack. Still bathed in sweat, pale and shaking, she returned to her husband and went home.

It took years and her third child's healthy growing up to restore Joan's confidence in herself as a mother.

## Separation Anxiety

Bobby, 17 months old, watched from the playpen in his grandmother's living room as his mother and father made ready to leave. Bobby couldn't say very many words yet, but he could recognize what was about to happen. Mommy put on her coat; Daddy searched in his pockets for keys. A great chunk of security and warmth was about to go out of the door. Just as Mommy and Daddy turned toward him for their good-by kiss, Bobby started to cry.

"Oh Gran, I'd hoped he wouldn't do this," said Mrs. B. "We've never left him for more than a few hours before and here we're going to be gone for two weeks."

"Don't worry, dear," soothed Gran. "I raised you all right and I can surely take care of little Bobby."

Mrs. B. tried to comfort Bobby with a hug, but was met only by yells and frantic clinging. The sound of his yells followed Mr. and Mrs. B. out the door.

Bobby's two week stay with Grandma was only sometimes pleasant. During the first week he often wandered through the house calling "Mamma." There were problems putting him to bed and generally he was fretful and crabby. During the second week he calmed down, playing quietly by himself much of the time. Grandma thought to herself how he'd go rushing to greet his Mommy when she returned.

The reality was different. Flushed and happy, Mommy came back. Bobby did not run to meet her when he heard her voice. She called his name, but he did not respond. She went over and picked him up. He scowled at her for interrupting his play.

Back home, for the next few days, Mrs. B. felt as if the bond of love between her son and herself had somehow weakened. Bobby seemed so detached. Over the next several days, however, she was relieved to find that Bobby had become his normal, demanding self. He was demanding, by the way, that she stay with him for a while. (This is a very normal reaction to separation from parents for children of this age.)

# LIVING WITH
# ANXIETY AND DEPRESSION

## *Anxiety Accompanying an Examination*

Dennis paced the floor. It was an idiotic, vicious circle, he thought. He was worried about his biology exam, next Friday. The only way he could pass was to study like crazy, but every time he sat down to study each word reminded him of the test. He'd start to get more and more nervous. The words seemed to stop at his eyes. They just didn't get through to his brain. He'd read a sentence ten times and not get the meaning. It seemed like it took an hour to read a page and then he couldn't remember two words of what he had read. "Good Lord," thought Dennis, "at this rate it'll take me a month to get through the chapter and the test is Friday." He decided to take a break. He got halfway down the hall toward the kitchen and then got even more worried, because he wasn't studying. He could feel the blood pounding in his temples, his thoughts raced, he couldn't concentrate, he could barely sit still. "I'm gonna blow it. I'm gonna blow it, I know it." Finally, Dennis decided to quit for the night, try to get some sleep, and start studying again tomorrow. He lay in his bed feeling as tight as a knot, hearing every drip and creak in the house. When he closed his eyes his mind filled with pictures of test tubes, paramesia, and disjointed phrases from his textbook. About 3 a.m. he finally fell asleep. It was a sleep full of unpleasant dreams. He awoke at 5 a.m., feeling like a moldy dishrag.

## Anxiety as an Everyday Experience

"O.K., now I've done it," thought Louise. The bank statement for Harold and Louise's joint checking account had arrived in the mail. Louise had discovered that Harold had written checks for about $200 worth of business expenses that she hadn't known about. And, of course, she, Louise, had just paid $62 for a dress and shoes that Harold didn't know about. "Dummy," she thought, "why can't I ever find anything I like at a place where we have a charge account." In her head, she figured that they were about $59 overdrawn. Now to sit down and figure it out for sure. "Two plus two and four makes seven, carry the one. Good grief. Two plus two and four are eight, carry nothing. No, Joey, Mommy can't get you a drink now. In a minute. Don't pester your mother. Stop that! Those are Mommy and Daddy's very important papers. Go outside and play. Joey, go away!" Louise worked, scrambling and unscrambling her sums, mislaying checks; in short, she was having a terrible time figuring the balance in her checkbook. A small lump like a piece of lead had settled in her stomach and her eyes felt tired looking at all the numbers. Suddenly, Louise jumped up, eyes bright and head clear. She felt good. She called Joey in for a snack and gave him a few extra cuddles. Not a worry in the world: $2.79 in the bank.

All the people mentioned above have experienced

feelings of anxiety and depression to greater or lesser degrees. For each, the distress and discomfort, be it for minutes, for years or forever, were as disabling as a physical injury, as human as laughter.

# CHAPTER TWO

# Anxiety and Depression: Symptoms and Severity

The balance between an individual's private mental world, his public behavior, his social world and the skin, bones and blood of his physical functioning is often a delicate one. The normal individual, in every phase of his life, meets and deals with anxieties and depressions. Like the normal people in the preceding chapter, he is more or less successful depending on the size of the task confronting him, his capabilities, his previous experience, and his well-being, both physical and mental. Even the strongest individual may be thrust deep into despair or frozen with inexplicable terrors given the appropriate circumstances. Some of these circumstances are well known: prolonged fatigue, bodily debilitation and confrontation with harrowing problems which appear to have no solutions. Likewise, the almost irrepressible buoyancy of the human personality has been well documented. For example, physicians and psychologists who have dealt with brain injuries cite the integrity of the individual's personality prior to the injury as one indicator of how well the person will function after the injury. In his moving book, *Death Be Not Proud*, author John Gunther tells how his son, having undergone several operations for the removal of a massive malignant brain tumor which left him crippled, bravely struggled to finish his science project and went on crutches to receive his high school diploma shortly before he died. How can we judge this boy's courage next to the courage of a neurotic who often sees the world through the smoky glasses of trauma, who gets up each morning with a dry mouth and trembling hands because he has to face a day of fears whose origins and ultimate effects elude him? Anxiety, as we shall see, in its extreme forms, can be as crippling as physical injury, incapacitating the individual for the business of life, keeping him a lonely, distraught invalid, or precipitating a total breakdown of his personality, with impairment of thought processes and disorganization of behavior.

In anxiety, there are two dimensions to severity: the character of each attack of anxiety and the frequency of occurrence. Does the individual become frozen with unbearable terror, does he flee in disorganized panic from he knows not what or does he merely feel butterflies in his stomach? Is each day and night an interminable battle with these feelings or does he experience this anxiety only once or twice a year?

In its milder forms, anxiety poses no real threat to the person or the integrity of his personality. Consider the case of Mrs. P. She is a young mother relatively new in the community. As she stands to ask a question and express an opinion at the local P. T. A., she feels her knees tremble slightly. She has some difficulty phrasing her question as she had it thought out, and her voice, at first, sounds drier and harsher than normal. She notes with surprise that she is gripping the back of the chair in front of her rather tightly. Her question over, she sits down. Her anxiety melts away as another parent rises to say that he felt her question was a good one. It lessens still more when the speaker agrees with her point, and it disappears as Mrs. P. notes friendliness and assent in the faces of those around her. Her brief anxiety may have been related to her seeking acceptance in the new community, to her ability to speak in front of others, to her desire to communicate a point of view that was important to her or to a combination of these and other factors. Her anxiety was brief; she was able to bring her shaking knees and cracking voice under control; the reaction of others was positive. Perhaps at the next meeting, anticipating a good reaction, she would find it even easier to speak and to assert herself. In technical terms, Mrs. P. had a transient adjustment reaction of the very mildest sort. The anxiety occurred in reaction to a clearly definable situation and disappeared as the situation changed. Mrs. P.'s experience is a common one. For many people, the occasions for anxiety are relatively infrequent, and the anxiety itself is mild. When stress and anxiety become a pounding, repetitive pattern, when each bout of fear and worry is a hair-raising experience in itself, the symptom picture may change radically. "The only thing there is to fear is fear itself" is a familar adage. Its truth is borne out when one looks at the lengths to which people will go to avoid or escape their own anxiety. Some neurotics develop their abnormal symptoms in reaction to anxieties which refuse to yield to "rational" methods of solution. A man with an inexplicable fear of closed-in spaces would walk up seven flights of stairs rather than take an elevator and experience panic. A prisoner in a concentration camp occupied his time by stealing tiny bits of leather and cloth from the prison guards and sewed himself a guard uniform rather than face, in his idle moments, the terror of admitting his total helplessness as a prisoner. The neurotic makes an uneasy truce with his anxieties at the cost of maintaining some symptoms and losing some freedom. However, he is able to go about his daily business and does not suffer any profound derangement of his personality. A psychotic, however, experiences radical change or disorganization of his personality structures, sometimes accompanied, in severe cases, by delusions, hallucinations, disordered thinking, grave depressions, extreme mood changes or bizarre behavior. Some psychotic reactions may be precipitated by a veritable tidal wave of anxiety. There is no better way to acquaint the reader with the possible effects of relentless anxiety than to relate some case histories of normals, neurotics and psychotics in which moderate or severe anxiety was a catalyst to crisis and a spur to symptom formation.

Mild anxiety may be characterized by an uneasy feeling and butterflies in the stomach. Moderate anxiety involves more general feelings of bodily tension and mental preoccupations. One of the things which may happen when a person "tenses up" is that he is more likely to react, positively or negatively, to anything and everything. In everyday terms, the person becomes very touchy. In psychological terms, the person's drive level is up, his perception is less acute, and his tendency to generalize is greater. When anxiety is severe, it becomes a total preoccupation and almost all phases of everyday functioning, such as sleeping, eating and moving, are affected.

## Frequent Mild Anxiety in a Normal Individual

Mark had a reputation on the block as being a nice guy, who was relatively friendly, but a little shy. If he was out mowing the lawn and a neighbor greeted him, he'd blush and stammer, say a few words, turn away, try to start the conversation again and then abruptly go back to his lawn mowing. He didn't know why social contacts with acquaintances seemed to upset him, but he always felt jumpy and unsure of himself in such situations. He would often say too much or too little, and it would make him feel hot and clammy. He was always glad when the other person finally went away.

## A Prolonged Attack of Moderately Severe Anxiety in a Neurotic

Arnold was beginning his second stage of study as a doctor. He had left his home and traveled across the country to begin his internship at a large, busy, eastern hospital. Unfortunately, the first service to which he was assigned was Physical Medicine and Rehabilitation. Each and every day he had to deal with people who had lost limbs, who had suffered paralyses, who had lost the power of speech, or whose bodily integrity had, in some way, been impaired. In medical school, he had worked with cadavers and seen sick people and had been only moderately and normally upset. Here, the effect was wholly different. Unconsciously, perhaps, a man with one leg was a powerful symbol to him of his own inadequacies and fears. The situation was aggravated by his being among strangers, far from friends and home.

The first day that Arnold went to work he felt an electric, disturbing uneasiness settle on him as he walked through the ward. He was tempted to stare, but already he felt he was being stared at and it would be unprofessional to stare back. All day he fidgeted. He was reprimanded by a senior staff member for not paying attention. He could not bring himself to eat in the hospital cafeteria; the food repelled him. Back home, he went to bed early and slept fitfully. At 6, he awoke with a start. He was flushed and pale and he felt as if there were a tight band across his chest. He could barely get his breath. He had had a nightmare, but couldn't remember anything about it. He cut his face when he shaved and his hand trembled so much that his hot morning coffee splashed his hand, scalding it. As he approached the hospital building, sweat broke out on his forehead. He walked around the building twice before going in. The day passed in misery.

The following weeks were much the same. Arnold had lost weight. He looked drawn and haggard from lack of sleep. He hadn't had a really decent night's sleep since he had come to this hospital. His ears rang; he felt lightheaded and vaguely nauseated. He had begun to spend more and more time in the labs and less and less time with the patients. His reports showed a lot of book work, but little thought. He had started to become preoccupied with safety and possible injury. He no longer drove his car, and when he walked up and down the stairs, he clung to the railings. He stopped smoking for fear of setting his mattress on fire. He washed very thoroughly after his visits to each patient and after every meal.

Three months after he had arrived, Arnold was due to be transferred to the Surgery service. By this time,

Arnold had a nice little set of phobias and compulsions. He left the hospital and returned home to recover and to make some decisions about his career.

## Severe Anxiety at the Onset of a Psychosis

On this particular morning, Marcia had received a letter from her grandmother. The letter explained how disappointed the family had been with the recent report of Marcia's grades. Marcia had been valedictorian of her high school class, but decided to leave the small town where she grew up and go to a large western university. Now she was earning average, but not outstanding, grades. Her grandmother wrote that sending Marcia to school, despite her scholarship, had jeopardized the family finances, and that if Marcia lost her scholarship, funding her education would lead to her mother and grandmother's living at the poverty level. Every word of the letter rang with accusation and disappointment.

Marcia folded the letter and placed it in a drawer. She looked downcast during lunch and left for her job at the library, leaving most of her meal untouched.

When Marcia came back from the library it was evident that something terrible had happened. A librarian had threatened to fire Marcia because she did not thoroughly check students' briefcases for stolen books. Marcia's reaction was panic. Maybe everything her grandmother had said about her was true, she thought. Maybe she didn't deserve confidence, respect or trust.

Marcia ran to see a friend. "Stay with me. I feel terrible, I don't know what's going to happen." Marcia began to cry and to pace. She couldn't sit still. She chewed at her nails and wrung her hands. She looked flushed and wild-eyed. She talked and talked about all the things which had been happening to her. She talked about her childhood, how her father had died, how her mother had changed. The words came out in great gushes. Marcia barely stopped for breath, as she jumped from one topic to another. Marcia's friend stayed up with her all that night. Sleep was an impossibility. By morning Marcia had lost her voice. Great tears slid down her cheeks. She tried to sit down, but jumped up in fear when she saw herself clawing at her own arms.

By noon Marcia was literally climbing the walls, crying, and scratching at the flowered wallpaper. Her speech had degenerated into incoherent babbling, and unhappy groans. Exhausted, she could not sleep; hungry, she could not eat. She could not go on. She just knew it. Something had to give. Yet she continued to pace, to roll on and off the bed. Her friend took her hand and told her that she was going to take her to the student health center. Marcia heard herself begin to shriek, to yell. Thought after thought spewed out of her head in disjointed sequence. She started to run. She found herself back in her dormitory room. Alone in her room, she spent another night like the first: without food, without sleep, without rest, without peace, without surcease. Her words were more wild than before. She spoke of enemies and conspiracies. Alarmed, her friends called the health service and asked for help. Marcia fought the sedative they gave her, fought the sleep, pulled at the straps that held her, until it finally became black.

## Depression: Symptoms and Severity

It is well known that depression affects an individual's mood, thoughts, behavior, appearance, bodily functions, and temporal perspective. The clinical symptoms of depression are more numerous, better documented, and more minutely described than those of anxiety. The pattern of the symptoms seem to be fairly consistent from individual to individual, varying in their manifestations only as the level of severity varies. For example, an indication of depression may involve merely a consistently pessimistic outlook in a normal individual or a fabrication of impending doom in a psychotic individual.

The mood of the depressed individual is one of sadness and unhappiness. He might feel that all the pleasure has gone out of life; he might ignore or overlook or cease to enjoy his usual sources of happiness. The mildly or moderately depressed person may have bouts of crying while a more severely depressed person might complain that he cannot cry.

The depressed person's thoughts focus on the black side of events. His outlook is pessimistic. He tends to downgrade himself, to feel guilty for real or imaginary wrongdoings and to expect failure and punishment since he feels he doesn't deserve anything better. His power of concentration declines and the efficiency of his thought decreases. There is a loss of interest in, and motivation for, his usual activities and goals. A lack of interest or an aversion to sex is common. In some cases, there is a preoccupation with thoughts of suicide. In many cases, even the most ordinary events are reinterpreted so as to become sources of worry. Thought often centers on the past; the person may ruminate about his past mistakes and hard times.

There is a tendency to neglect one's personal appearance, both in regard to clothing and grooming, and in regard to facial expressions and gestures. The face may seem wooden with a mirthless smile pasted across it. In most cases, the tempo of bodily movements slows down. Every motion seems effortful. Even speech may be affected; in very severe instances, the person may cease to talk; in more normal cases, getting a reply from a depressed person might seem "like pulling teeth." In some instances, the depression is accompanied by agitation. Instead of slowing down, the person becomes nervous, wringing his hands, pacing, etc.

Often the agitation and effortful movement alternate.

The general languor of bodily movement is reflected in the "interior" of the depressive as well. The whole digestive system seems to slow down. There is loss of appetite, loss of weight, and constipation. In severe cases, a person might not have a bowel movement for weeks, or complain that he feels he is "rotting inside." Sleeping problems, such as difficulty falling asleep, waking without feeling rested, and nightmares, may also occur. In a number of mild cases, the picture is reversed: The individual complains of overeating and oversleeping. For some women, the menstrual cycle may become lengthened or may even stop for many months. Vague aches and pains are common. The depressed individual may complain of such things as headaches, a feeling of tightness in the chest, or stomach upset.

For the depressed personality, life may become a bleak, black, bitter experience. Neither in sleep nor in waking may he find enjoyment. Suicide attempts, threats of suicide, and thoughts of suicide may be the result.

### A Mild Case of Depression
### in a Normal Individual

Henry had been awake since 4. He felt tired and told himself he needed more rest. "It'd be just like you to fall back asleep and oversleep. You'd be late for your appointment at 10 and there'd be no chance of your getting the job," he thought, "not that you could get it if you tried. You lost your last job. A lot of people were laid off, but you were one of the first. You didn't do so well in high school either. No chance for college. I guess Jane would have been better off with Tom after all. I bet he's never failed at anything." The voice in Henry's head continued in this vein for several hours, dredging up every possible misdeed, every minor vice or failing that Henry had ever had. To hear the voice, one would find it hard to believe that Henry had been a top mechanic for a major aerospace company. Like so many others he had lost his job as the industry had closed down section after section in reaction to economic pressure.

Jane nudged Henry: "It's seven o'clock, dear. Hadn't you better get started?"

Henry did not reply, he merely looked at her accusingly. His inner voice took over again. "So she doesn't trust you to get up by yourself. 'You'll be late for school, sweetie.' It was the same way she would talk to a kid. But you aren't up, are you? You just want to lie here, don't you? It'd make you happy just to stay in bed. No job. Jane'd have to go to work. What kind of man are you? What difference does it make, anyway? This interview is going to fall through, too. It doesn't matter if you stay here or go. 'Thank you, we'll call you.' The door shuts and the personnel man says, 'Well that does it. We have three openings and

40 men have applied. I'd rate this guy number 39. He was one of the first that Conjet let go, and he sure doesn't show much spirit. He was 10 minutes late to begin with.' "

Henry's reverie was interrupted by the ring of the phone. He let Jane answer it. Excitedly, she handed it to him.

"What? There must be some mistake. Yes, that's how you spell it. I worked there. You sure? O.K., O.K." Henry put down the phone and, stunned, looked at Jane. "I've got the job. The interview's a formality. Their new section head was from Conjet. He insisted that I be foreman."

The voice in his head began, "You lucked out. You never would have made it by yourself. You're still in bed, aren't you?"

Jane, her eyes wet, gave him a big hug. Surprised, he found himself hugging back and found, with a jolt, that she felt strange and new in his arms. "She still loves me," he thought. "She has all along. I've barely paid her any attention for weeks." The accusing voice in his head began to get laryngitis. He recognized that he was hungry, and despite his own wishes, he'd better get up and get started if he was going to have a decent breakfast and get to the interview on time. At that moment, the accusing inner voice packed his bag, removing the lead weights he had placed on Henry's back, and left. Henry lept out of bed.

## Moderately Severe Depression
### in a Neurotic Individual

Eleanor sat in the doctor's office, waiting for the doctor to return with the results of the examination. It had taken her nearly 20 minutes to dress and the doctor had busied himself with another patient.

Her hair was dishevelled; she had forgotten to smooth it. Her blouse was buttoned crookedly, her skirt was creased and slightly soiled. As she sat in the chair, she slumped forward, her hands crossed limply on her knees. Her face looked pale and expressionless. As the doctor entered, she pulled her mouth into a tight grimace which passed for a smile. She did not greet him. He waited an uncomfortable minute for her to speak. When she didn't, he did. She had heard it all before. Nothing important was the matter. Low blood pressure. Very slight anemia. She looked run down, but maybe she just needed a rest. She spoke briefly. "Perhaps the anemia is more serious than your simple tests showed." He shook his head. She clamped her mouth shut, determined not to speak again if he was going to show such discourtesy. Doctors didn't care about people anymore, she thought. They never make house calls. She had literally had to drag herself here. Who knows what could have happened to her on the way? Her son had refused to stay home from work to drive her to the doctor. She could have stayed home and died of neglect for all he cared. If she'd fallen while crossing the street, she would never have had the strength to get up again. She probably would have been hit by a car, and no one would have cared. Well, she must not have been a very good mother to raise such a son. Now she was paying for it. She told her son so this morning, and he had just turned away. That proved it. She was no good to anyone any more. Not even the doctors would help her. They didn't think she was worth the time to save. She took the doctor's prescripton for the laxative, slowly folded it twice, and looked at him as though he had betrayed her. She opened her pocketbook, undid the zippered compartment, put the paper inside, zipped the zipper and snapped the pocketbook shut. With effort, she got up and left. "I'll just go home and die. It's all that's left for me. I am so sick and there's not one soul who is concerned about it." When her son came home, she told him there was nothing anyone could do to help and went to her room, leaving him puzzled and upset.

## Severe Depression in a Psychotic

Harold knew they would be coming for him soon. He was frightened, but that was O.K., he deserved it. If it hadn't been for him, the world wouldn't be in the state it was now. He had read in the paper about the blond man, 45 years old, who had fallen in front of a subway train. Harold was sure that this man had been the store clerk who, 26 years ago, had given him too much change. Undoubtedly, this led to a life of crime and now the suicide. Harold felt like a murderer. In fact he felt he always had been. His wife must have died prematurely because of his neglect. She must have found out about his shady business dealings and died of a broken heart. His daughter never married. That was because Harold was such a miserable, cold father. She probably thought all men were like him. He remembered forgetting her birthday. Oh, how callous he was.

The government would be coming soon. He hoped they'd hurry. He charged too much when he'd sold groceries. He wondered if anyone had starved in that neighborhood because of him and guessed probably they had. Oh, Lord! He remembered, he'd forgotten to pay the electricity bill before they'd moved him here. The water in the pipes would freeze. His daughter could never pay for the damage. She'd be destitute. How could he do this to other people? He knew he didn't deserve to live. No torture would be too terrible. He wished they'd hurry and come. The world would be better without him.

To the nurse, Harold seemed so mild and quiet. He sat there day after day saying nothing, looking worried. She thought soon they'd have to feed him intravenously because he'd lost so much weight. It was a shame no one came to visit him, but then, his wife and daughter had died years ago.

## LIVING WITH
## ANXIETY AND DEPRESSION

Anxiety and depression can envelop and strangle one's life, or they can be normal reactions to normal problems. Their roots in the human personality are deep. In the next chapter, the nature and origins of these reactions will be discussed.

CHAPTER THREE

# About Anxiety

You have been introduced in this book to people who have experienced, to some degree, psychological distress, the pain of anxiety, the torment of depression. You have been provided with a description of the symptoms which typically mark off, in the eyes of the diagnostician, mild from severe states of anxiety, and mild from severe depressions. Undoubtedly, anxiety and depression are not foreign to you. Sometimes it seems impossible to get through the week, the day, the hour in one piece. Sometimes you want to kill, sometimes cry, sometimes both at once. You worry. Over money. Over your job. Over your husband. Over your wife. You worry about your children, your age, or your health. Or whether you are doing the right thing. In truth, we live in a world in which frustration is ever present; failure is ever present. Disaster is ever possible. Hate is cheap. Loneliness is cheap. Disinterest is cheap. Love and caring are extremely dear.

Many have difficulty in surviving. Many have difficulty in living a decent life, and few live the good life.

## LIVING WITH
## ANXIETY AND DEPRESSION

When things are not going well, we confront anxiety, we experience depression. What is worse, anxiety and depression all too often make it impossible to roll with, to adapt to, or to get over life's insults, whether real or imagined. When one is afraid to make a move, one often stands still. When one does not believe that he can cope, he often does not try to cope. When one does not have the energy to resist, one is overwhelmed.

When confronted by an enemy, it is frequently useful to seek to understand its nature, to collect intelligence about it before undertaking a defense against its threats or an attack against its weak points. What, then, is the nature of anxiety? How is it best to campaign against it?

Psychologists are likely to contrast anxiety with fear. The comparison is an apt one, as far as it goes. An individual is said to be fearful if frightened by a real, external threat.

You see the bank statement. You know you will be overdrawn this month. You have issued the "bad" checks. One is for the rent, one is for the market, and the third is for tickets to the Policeman's Ball. You know you will never be able to cover the checks, and so you are frightened.

You are relaxing in the bathtub and hear a scream from your child. You are frightened.

The note says "Bring all of your records to this Internal Revenue Service Office at 9:00 A.M. on 17 June. . . ." You did not declare your tips, or your bonus, or you have lost your records. You are worried.

The night is cold and rainy; it feels as though the chill has gotten into your bones and has decided to stay a while. You are tired and a bit groggy. The day has been long. You notice there is no one else on the street. Your home is still a couple of blocks away. Suddenly, from between two houses, a man quickly moves toward you. You know you do not know him. You know that he is going to mug you. You feel panic.

You are up for a new job. You know that there are many candidates and few positions. You are older than most applicants. A hesitancy, a jumpiness rises from your gut as you are led to the interview.

The examination will be a beast. You want to get into graduate school. You are afraid.

He looks seven feet tall, weighs two hundred pounds, and smells of booze. He pushes ahead of you in line. You are waiting for a subway and the crowd starts pushing.

The doctor steps out of his office and motions to you. He is holding the results of the lab test.

Fear is one of the emotions that we often experience in reaction to a recognized, real, external threat to our well-being.

Fear has its use, its purpose. It puts us on guard, and prepares us for action. When danger is upon us, both body and mind prepare for the emergency. The body's resources are put into readiness for swift action, to fight or flee. The heart begins to pump blood more quickly and with a stronger beat, so that more blood will be sent to the lungs. Breathing deepens, and within the lungs, the bronchi dilate, making for greater efficiency in the transfer of oxygen from the air to the body. The increase in oxygen will be needed for the increased demands placed upon the body by stress. Sugar is released by the liver to provide the muscles with more energy to burn. Blood flow is altered. More blood goes to the muscles and brain, less to the skin and to the gut. The supply of lymphocytes, white blood cells which aid the body in repairing injury and staunching infection, increases in the blood stream. You have undoubtedly felt the force of these preparations after a near accident when driving or just before a fight.

While the body is organizing for action, the mind is also preparing itself. In searching for a plan to avoid danger, in searching for a way to master it, the mind may, in a period of alarm, not notice the action that is being taken by the body. Only after the danger is past may an individual be aware of his own exertions. Both mind and body are readied for action.

Though fear has its use, too much of a good thing is often not a good thing. Fear may breed cowardice as well as strength. Fear may prepare us for constructive action or lead us to panic. Fear may strengthen our body, or if it persists long enough, exhaust it. What we do in fear may be more destructive than the danger itself would have been. People in panic are often very dangerous people, dangerous to themselves and to others. How many people die in panic, crushed beneath the mob? How often do individuals needlessly injure themselves or others in reacting excessively to real but mild danger? To be useful, fear must be kept within bounds; it must warn and not control, prepare but not exhaust; it must be appropriate to the situation, and it must set the stage for appropriate action.

While psychologists tend to label the individual's response to external threat *fear*, they call the individual's response to threat from within *anxiety*. Anxiety has often been described as the experience of fear without real danger being present. The person who worries over nothing, the woman who becomes uncomfortable at the mere mention of the word "rat," a man afraid of heights, a woman who experiences overwhelming apprehension, who knows something is about to happen, who has a premonition of impending doom, are said to know the experience of anxiety.

Anxiety, like fear, is intended to serve a useful purpose. Anxiety acts to warn the personality that it is stressed, that defensive action must be taken. For example, anxiety may be experienced in contexts in which a person is tempted to act in a manner which is inconsistent with his or her moral sense. When the individual anticipates the rebuke of his conscience, the feelings of guilt which he knows will follow, and the loss of his self-esteem, he feels what is known as moral anxiety. Anxiety may also be produced by the fear that an urge or desire will become uncontrollable, or that the basic needs of the individual will never be satisfied adequately.

While fear and anxiety are often treated by psychologists as separate entities, they have so much in common that they are hardly distinguishable. Both serve to warn that all is not right, that quick change must occur. Both move the individual to a state of readiness. Both prepare him to cope with threat. Even the most obvious differences between the two seem to break down under close scrutiny. Who is to say what is a real and what is an imagined threat? What is a reaction to internal stress and what is a reaction to external threat? What does the crime rate have to be before one is realistically afraid to walk down a dark street alone instead of being neurotically preoccupied with rape? Is fear of enclosed spaces, claustrophobia, a reflection of a struggle for power within the personality, or a learned emotional reaction following an experience that an individual has actually had? For our purpose, it is quite satisfactory, with one major qualification, to view anxiety as being more or less identical in nature to fear, and thus to consider anxiety and fear to be synonymous. The proviso is that we recognize that the source of anxiety may not be obvious at first glance, or if it is obvious, that others may not agree that the individual should be afraid. Why should anyone be afraid of riding in elevators, be uncomfortable about sleeping in someone else's bed, or using someone else's bathroom? Why should anyone fear old age? Why should people awaken every morning knowing they are doomed, when nothing unusual has happened to them in the last fifteen years?

Unfortunately, not being able to identify what one is afraid of or having other people fail to appreciate the danger that one fears may have dire consequences: a person could quickly get a reputation for weirdness. He or she might even be considered crazy or consider themselves to be crazy. Considering the way we treat the people in this society that we consider to be crazy, insanity is a label we can all do without. If a person were not anxious enough before, having people begin to look at him strangely or act toward him as if he were something less than human is guaranteed to help him come undone. Just as likely a danger is that the individual who is anxious will not be able to cope with the threat he fears, the threat that is causing him anxiety, because he may not even recognize what, indeed, the danger is. How can one cope with what one cannot see, or touch? How can one plan a course of action against an unknown enemy? How can one avoid wondering why his heart is pounding, his breathing is rapid, the palms of his hands are sweating, when there is no good reason, or seems to be no good reason, to be afraid?

## LIVING WITH
## ANXIETY AND DEPRESSION

What happens when a person does not come to grips with that which provokes his fears? A number of things can happen, none of them comfortable or pleasant. Under prolonged stress, for example, a massive shutdown of those bodily activities which promote growth, adequate sexual responsiveness, and even resistance to infection may occur. Finding oneself sexually inadequate is not likely to help a marriage on the rocks or to bolster a sagging sense of self-esteem. Finding oneself too tired to pull oneself out of bed is not likely to make it any easier to get the house-work done. Finding oneself always on edge is not likely to make it easier to feel comfortable with people, or to make new friends. Being anxious all or most of the time is not likely to bring peace to a sick stomach. If the stress is persistent and severe, exhaustion may ensue, perhaps leading to death.

So devastating, so evil is the effect of prolonged or severe anxiety on the individual, the mind often employs a number of defensive maneuvers to minimize its impact. These are well known to mental health professionals because these defensive reactions often lead to neurotic symptoms. The most frequently used defense against anxiety is probably repression. The principle of repression is simply stated: "What you don't know won't hurt you." In repression, anything that might produce anxiety is automatically and habitually excluded from awareness. When repression is employed, a "Berlin Wall" or "Iron Curtain" separates threatening material from consciousness. "Hear no evil; see no evil; speak no evil" is another way of putting it. The problems inherent in this tactic are obvious. For one, keeping the dike intact requires effort, effort that could be spent elsewhere. For another, putting your head in the sand rarely solves problems and often makes them worse. Because this defense operates automatically and habitually, the individual, after a while, loses the ability to cope with his problems because he has never had the opportunity to learn what they are.

One of the most dramatic examples of the harm that the pervasive use of repression can bring about is found in the condition termed *hysteria*. Hysterics "give up" part of themselves to avoid experiencing anxiety. Eyesight, hearing, the use of an arm or a leg, each might be sacrificed to avoid the pain that fear produces.

Cynthia was twenty-five and unmarried when she came to the clinic because she could not see. There was no physical reason for it. She impressed everyone as being a pleasant person, very prim and proper. She had good things to say about everyone, trusted everyone, and never seemed to get angry. She said she rarely got upset. In fact, she did not even seem to be too much bothered by her blindness. As her story unfolded, it appeared as if she was the ideal child, the

**47**

only child of older, very strict parents. They did not tolerate "wrong" behavior, and she quickly learned to be a good child, for if she were bad she was punished severely. Love was dependent upon good behavior. When she was bad, she was an orphan, and she really needed to be loved. Bad behavior was being "dirty," having "dirty" thoughts, doing "dirty" things, and any expression of anger was not to be tolerated. Sex was dirty; anything having to do with the relationship between men and women was taboo. She began to menstruate at twelve. Menstruation came as a shock to her, because nobody had prepared her for it, and she had no idea about what was happening to her. She had few friends to tell her the "facts of life." Other children were too rough, it seemed, and she was not allowed to associate with them. Sex education was not part of her curriculum.

Now, for better or worse, it is almost impossible not to be smothered by sex, inundated by sex. Sex leaps out at us in the movies, on television, in books, in the way people talk, in the way they dress. Sexual stimuli are almost impossible to avoid. Cynthia tried. She was a good girl, and good girls, she had been taught, do not think about sex. She minimized the impact of sex in her life by trying to avoid those things which stimulated "dirty" thoughts in her mind; she avoided those things by learning not to see them. Cynthia *learned* to be blind. She did not worry much about being blind;

being blind had its use: being blind "protected" her from coming to grips with her own sexuality.

There are other defenses employed against anxiety. They go by different names—*projection, rationalization, denial, isolation, undoing, suppression*—but they all serve the same purpose: to avoid anxiety without dealing adequately with it. When used in excess, these defenses end up in defending against health and producing maladjustment.

The origins and etiology of the experience of anxiety are quite unclear at this point in time, and accounts of those origins are clearly speculative. Some have argued that our first experience with anxiety occurs when we are infants, helpless to control our own destiny, our well-being completely in the hands of others and we, ourselves, totally and hopelessly overstimulated by our environment and our inner needs. A few have suggested that the trauma of being born is the prototype of all future anxiety states. Yet others have turned to the notion that *primary anxiety* is linked to the fear of abandonment. Whatever theories are advanced to account for the origin of anxiety in man, it is clear that man experiences anxiety whenever he believes that any object which is important to his survival as he is now is threatened. Man fears and becomes anxious about threats to his way of living, or to the way he would like to be living. He may become anxious about, or fear, even the most seemingly trivial event or object, if that event or object is, represents, or symbolizes an attack on his way of life, his self-esteem, his values, or his future plans.

The question to ask, therefore, when you find yourself worried, anxious, or fearful is "What important goals of mine are under attack?" and "What do I stand to lose?" The answers to those questions, in their particulars, are different for each of us, but in general, for most of us, living within the culture that we do, we are going to respond that we most fear that our actions will alienate our loved ones, will make it impossible for us to be loved, will indicate to ourselves or others that we are, indeed, inadequate, incompetent, or evil.

Cynthia feared that she would be considered "immoral." She learned that whenever she engaged in "dirty" behavior or had "dirty" thoughts, or whenever she embarked on a course of action that her parents considered evil, they withdrew their love and attention from her. To them, she ceased to exist. To be abandoned was the ultimate catastrophe for Cynthia. Anything was better than that. For her, it was better to be blind than not to exist in the eyes of those who mattered most. For Cynthia, it was better to be blind than to bear the almost overwhelming anxiety that she associated with the threat of abandonment. Of course, Cynthia was an unusual person. She had an unusual childhood, leading to an unusual adulthood. But the same principles that apply to Cynthia apply to us, also. Perhaps these principles manifest themselves in less dramatic fashion, but they apply, nonetheless. We become fearful, or become anxious, when we believe that we are in danger of losing something that is important to us.

# CHAPTER FOUR

# About Depression

When psychologists talk about depression, their talk most frequently centers around three topics —loss, character development, and the frustration-aggression hypothesis. The importance of this triad to the understanding of depression can be traced to Freud's classic paper "Mourning and Melancholia," which was written in 1917. In that essay, Freud compared the depressive experience with the usual, and quite normal, reaction that people have to the loss of a loved one or a cherished ideal. When we lose a loved one, the world becomes a sadder place in which to live. We lose a good bit of the zest we had for life, even if that loss is only temporary. When we awaken in the morning, there is less reason to get out of bed. An important part of our lives has gone. There is one less person who cares for us. There is one less person to call on the phone, to argue with, to enjoy, and to have coffee with. There is one less person to love, one less person to love us. By necessity, the mind of the bereaved becomes focused upon the past. To think about the future reminds him of his loss. Thinking about the past enables him to hold on to, to cherish the joys, to taste the pain, to savor the pleasure, and to retain in some small measure the life of the departed.

The death of others also serves to remind us of our own vulnerability. We too will not live forever, a sobering thought. Death reminds us that our life also has an end. We ask ourselves, have we lived enough, long enough, well enough, accomplished enough to shuck off life today, or tomorrow? Who will mourn our passing? Was it all worth it? Does it really matter? Do *I* matter? Who will replace my love? No one really can, no one ever could. Who will take care of me as they did? No one.

But for most people life goes on. It must. New interests arise, new distractions. Perhaps, just perhaps, we can live forever. The old invulnerability returns, but perhaps in a more subdued form. Small changes are made, a new hobby, a vow to lead a better, fuller life. Life goes on, at least until the next time we are brought up short.

Unlike bereavement, in which the world of the aggrieved seems to be less full and less worthwhile, depression makes the individual himself feel empty and worthless. In depression, it is not the world that is felt to be defective and full of woe, but the individual. The depressive may not have lost his love, the object of his attention, in reality. It is sufficient that he lose it psychologically. No one need really die; the threat of separation is sufficient to plunge the depressive into a bottomless well of despair. A "falling-out" is equivalent, in the depressive's mind, to the death of a loved one. A shrug, a glance, the wrong word at the wrong time, the right word at the wrong time, any hint of rejection, and dejection will soon follow. Rejection, imagined or not, leads to sadness, worry, exhaustion, and self-deprecation.

The vulnerability of the depressive to loss, real or imagined, was attributed by Freud to a particular form of character development. Freud believed that early in life, during infancy in fact, the child came to view the world predominantly in one of two ways. The infant could accept the reality of the world, accept the notion that others existed in their own right, a path which led to normal development; or the infant could believe that he or she was the "be-all" and "end-all" of existence. Freud called the latter attitude *narcissism*. Most of us refer to this as "being self-centered." There is a good deal of the narcissist in all of us. How many times, for example, have other people seemed to you to be part of a dream, your dream, and all that was necessary to alter the script was for you to turn over and start again? The important thing to bear in mind, however, is that in the narcissistic personalities this attitude is automatically employed. There is no thought about it, no deliberation, no choice. It is the way things are going to be. It is the right and proper way for things to be.

There are many consequences of narcissistic character development. Two are of prime importance to our understanding of depression. The first is that the ties of the narcissist to others are quite tenuous. Remember, he feels that others do not exist in their own right. Whenever frustrated, the narcissist tries to start the dream all over again, often with a new set of characters. Those who have frustrated him no longer exist. Understandably, under those circumstances, the narcissist forms few deep and lasting relationships. To others, narcissists are unpredictable people, difficult to get along with. They love you one minute and hate you the next. They give others very little over the long run. Such relationships and such friendships as narcissists form are by their nature fragile. Secondly, since the narcissist believes that only he exists, believes that only he controls his destiny, that he is accountable only to himself, the only person the narcissist can blame for his failures is himself. When his life is going well, when he is satisfied with his dream, the narcissist rides high. When his wishes are frustrated, the narcissist becomes depressed. This depression stems from the narcissist's anger at his frustration. This anger is turned against himself, for there is no one else that the narcissist can blame for his misfortune.

Freud believed that frustration naturally led to aggression. This conjecture of Freud's has been termed the frustration-aggression hypothesis. Frustration arises whenever an important activity of the individual is thwarted. Frustration occurs whenever a goal is blocked. The degree of frustration the individual experiences, small or great, is determined by the importance to the individual of the aim which he finds himself unable to achieve. Freud, of course, focused his attention on what he considered to be instinctual goals. He concerned himself with what happened, for example, when sexual behavior was thwarted. But, whenever a person meets with frustration, anger arises.

You need a new pair of shoes, for example, but the budget will not handle it. Frustration leads to aggression.

You expect a promotion that does not materialize. You feel anger.

You miss your train, bus, or ride. You feel anger.

You ask a friend for a favor and are refused. You feel anger.

You need love and attention and do not receive either. You become angry.

You coordination is not as good as it once was, your eyesight is failing, and you feel the best days are over. You expect respect or, at least, consideration, and get none. You need understanding and have no one to whom to turn. You expect sympathy and receive rebuke.

In each of these instances, your plans, your hopes, or your expectations are frustrated and your anger builds. You must express that anger in some way, and, if you are the narcissistic type, you turn your anger inward, against yourself. You hate yourself for what you have done. You wish to punish yourself for the harm you have inflicted upon yourself. You rage against yourself. What kind of a person could have produced such misery? Only an evil, stupid child, a dirty, corrupt, selfish, disgusting animal. Who is that child? Who is that animal? Who is it that has spoiled your plans, upset your life? The answer that comes to you is, of course, you yourself. The extreme of such self-punishment is suicide.

Suicide is a decision about life. The suicide believes that there is no profit in going on. Whatever happens tomorrow is not going to be a major improvement over what went on yesterday and what is going on today. Taxes will go up. The amount of money left to spend will go down. Somewhere they are still bombing the jungle. Friends have died and will continue to do so. In far parts of the world, and even in this country, people are starving to death. Cancer lives; people die. A new disease is cured; another disease is discovered. There is war, there always has been, there always will be. There is hate and injustice, there always has been, and there always will be. While suicide is a decision about life, it is more often a decision about the person who is living it. The suicide believes that there is no profit in going on. In addition to his disbelief in a better tomorrow, the suicide often experiences the feeling that he is unloved and uncared for. He often believes that he is not worthy of life, that he is a bother to others, and that because of the way he is, he cannot change.

The surety with which the suicide knows that nothing is going to get better for him has its source in his narcissism. Since he alone controls his destiny, and since he feels he cannot change, there is no hope. The pain and despair that the suicide feels may be attributed to the anger he feels against those who frustrate him. He turns his anger against himself.

While Freud has certainly presented us with an exceptional framework on which to build our understanding of depression, there has been, over the years, some extension and revision of his views. The importance of loss, character development, and frustration to depression are still recognized, but a reinterpretation of those concepts has taken place.

People become depressed when they lose someone or something that is of value to them. The more important the loss, the more likely one is to experience depression. Why is that so? The answer is not terribly difficult nor complicated. Let us analyze what the loss of a loved one may mean. When one loves someone, he shares his life with that person—they share a kind of destiny and they are close to each other. People can get a great deal of pleasure from others and especially, hopefully, from those whom they love. The amount of social interchange between those who love each other is enormous. They sleep together, eat together, talk with each other, watch television together and go to the movies together. They share jobs around the house or apartment, share values with each other, share expenses, and tell each other what is right and what is wrong. In sum, they give pleasure to each other and regulate each other. When we lose someone whom we love, we literally lose much of value in our life. That loss is enough to depress even the strongest of us.

Depression is also a natural consequence of lost ideals and lost opportunities. For years, a student whom I know subjected himself to the most rigorous studies, giving up many of the pleasures that other adolescents had, in order to prepare himself for admission to medical school. In fact, through the last two years of high school and through four years of college, he had little else but his books, his exams, his papers, and his dreams. He knew that when he was a physician he would help people, he would work very hard, and he would live with respect, dignity, and in relative affluence. He would marry well. He would marry someone who would take pride in him, raise his children, and work beside him. However, he was not admitted to medical school. He became depressed. Until he found new pleasures, new hopes, and a new way to live, his life would be relatively empty of meaning.

## Depression Accompanying Physical Disability

John worked as an over-the-road truck driver. He made good money, had a nice house, and was proud of his family. His son had become quite a basketball player. John was a sports freak. When he wasn't watching a football game, a baseball game or a basketball game, he was watching a tennis match, or a golf tournament, though he really did not have the same passion for those upper-class sports that he had for football. Every Wednesday night, when he was in town, he played cards with the boys. Poker, beer, and good friends, with no women around; these were the ingredients necessary for a great evening. Things were really going well for John until he began to lose his eyesight. The physician he saw expressed sympathy for him. He told him in the nicest and most considerate way possible that he was going to be blind. John appreciated the kindness that the eye-doctor had shown him, but he knew that kindness would not restore his sight. John knew that good wishes would not give him a pay check. Good wishes could not undo John's feelings that he had lost his life.

## Depression in Bereavement

Mrs. Thompson's husband died suddenly. There was no time to prepare for it. He was only fifty-five when a heart attack struck him down. They had been married for twenty-seven years. Though they never had any children, though they did not have many close friends, they had each other. He had left her well taken care of financially. She had the house free and clear, and there was enough in the way of insurance to keep her comfortable. Her husband had taken pains to see that everything was always in order. He knew how to take care of her, and he did it well. She never wrote a check in her life. She never had to do much of anything, except keep house and keep her husband happy. Now he was gone, and she was alone. Who would not feel depression in such a circumstance? Who would not feel the gaping void, the hole inside of him, when placed in such unfortunate circumstances? Who would be happy about starting a new life at fifty-five? Who would get pleasure out of giving up so much that was important to him? Who could not sympathize with Mrs. Thompson's depression?

While it is obvious that a great loss may lead to depression, it is also true that some people adjust to that loss relatively well while others never quite regain their past level of success in living. Further, while depression is understandable when one experiences great personal loss, it is not so clear why some people become depressed in circumstances in which their loss appears to others to be trivial. Freud attempted to resolve these issues by introducing the concept of narcissism. But there may be a simpler and more straightforward way to understand the idiosyncratic response of the individual to real or threatened loss.

Let us begin the process of understanding depression with a few simple assumptions. For one, it seems reasonable to presume that the greater the loss, the more likely and more severe will be the depression that follows it. How does one measure the severity of loss? By estimating the extent of adjustment necessary to cope with that loss. How many new habits will have to be learned? How many old habits will have to be forgotten? How much effort will be necessary to "make good" that loss? How many alternative ways does the individual have to regain some of that which was lost? If one puts all of his eggs in one basket, and that basket is lost, one has little with which to start over again, especially if one needs to have eggs to be happy, and there are no more eggs to be found. A person with one companion with whom she has shared everything stands to lose far more when that companion departs than one who has shared many interests with many people. A woman who invests her whole life in raising her children may well become depressed when her last child leaves the house to strike out on his own. Why else is there so much crying at weddings? The loss of a thousand dollars is likely to have more dire consequences than the loss of one dollar, unless, of course, the person who loses the dollar loses his last dollar, and the person who loses the thousand dollars is a millionaire.

Often a signal that a great loss is coming may be sufficient to provoke depression. This fact accounts for many episodes of depression that at first glance may seem irrational to an independent and "objective" observer. A forgotten anniversary may be taken by a wife to mean that her husband no longer cares for her, no longer loves her. Someone who is insecure is likely to be searching for danger signals, and is also more likely to find them, even when they do not exist, than one who is confident. When you know that eight people in your division are going to be fired and you may be one of them, it is amazing how sensitive you can be to the tone of your manager's voice or the look on his face.

How secure an individual feels in the face of threat depends upon many factors. Among them are how severe the threat is, how successful the individual has been in coping with similar threats in the past, how much support from others the individual may reasonably count on to deal with the threat, and how comfortable and confident the person feels about himself. If he has frequently failed in the past, it is likely that he will feel that he will fail again, whether circumstances warrant that fear or not. If every attempt a person has made to establish meaningful contact with others has failed in the past, he is very probably going to be worried about the likelihood that any future relationship will be successful, no matter how often and in how many ways he is told that he is going to succeed at last.

The life stance that a person has developed is also likely to determine the success with which he will deal with loss. Some people have learned from their very earliest years to live life passively. This is especially true of women in our society. Women are taught that to seek life's goals aggressively is "improper," or "unfeminine." They are taught to let things happen to them. It is the man's job to provide for them financially. It is the man's role to have a career. It is the man who is supposed to actively seek sexual gratification. Men are supposed to be active and searching; women are supposed to be receptive and submissive. The man lives for his job, and the woman lives for her man. This is all well and good, until the woman loses her man. In too many cases, all she has been trained to do is to sit tight and wait for someone else to take care of her. If no one appears on the horizon, she is left to her own inadequately-developed coping devices, left to take care of herself without being adequately prepared to do so. Is it any wonder that people who live life passively are less likely to bounce back, more likely to be susceptible to depression than those who are accustomed to fending for themselves?

In addition to the sense of loss and the lack of interest in living that depressives often experience, self-hate is also common. Rebuke for misdeeds often fills their thoughts. Sometimes it seems as if the depressive is willing to take responsibility for all of his own failings and those of everyone else, but is unable to take credit for any success. The responsibility for failure which a person who feels depressed is willing to assume often reaches monumental and pathetically funny proportions. In cases of severe depression, depression frequently requiring hospitalization, it is not unusual for the depressive to feel that he is so contaminated by his own foulness that he will infect and thereby kill anyone with whom he comes into contact. Extreme? Perhaps, but the process that led to this bizarre idea is the same as that which in relatively less severe depressions leads one to believe such notions as "everything I do is wrong," or "I am just no good," or "no one cares about me." In relatively mild depressions, common self-deprecations are, "I am stupid," "I am ugly," "I am not fit to be in decent company," "I will always foul up a good thing," and on, and on, and on.

Self-misuse is, more often than not, a matter of habit, a habit built upon a foundation of excessive expectations of one's self and the acquired tendency to turn anger inward. Both are generally learned when a child is quite small and continue to be reinforced throughout adulthood. While "a man's reach should exceed his grasp" is true for some matters, if that adage is applied to each of a man's activities, he is more likely to be led to the gates of hell than of heaven. If nothing is good enough, then one is doomed to frustration. One can never be satisfied and one can never rest. This is especially the case when the individual has not learned to tell himself "enough is enough," "I'm not superman," or whatever other signals he might use to slow down his headlong rush into absurd perfectionism. "Just do as well as you can," if really meant, is a terrible admonition, and, if it is intended as an excuse, it can be done without. How do you know when you have done your best? If you feel any reserve left, if you feel you could go on, well then, you haven't done your best. You have only done your best when you have failed, when you have pushed the limit and realized that you could do no more. Done your best about what? About cleaning a dirty ashtray when your husband needs your attention? Clearly, doing your best and not having a sense of proportion about what effort should be exerted in what activities is likely to do the individual, and those that he comes into contact with, more ill than good.

## Depression and Perfectionism

Mrs. McGuire, no one ever called her Molly, ran a tight ship. Not a speck of dust in the house. Not an ash in an ashtray. My God, she even waxed the inside of her mailbox. Everything had its place, and everything was in order. If you asked her why she was always tired, that is, if you could get her to sit down long enough before dusting for the fourth or fifth time before leaving for mass, she would tell you "from working so hard." And, if you asked why she was working so hard, she would mumble something about being "brought up right," the "good of the family," or "that's a woman's job." She neglected to point out, however, that she was constantly irritated by her husband and only child (it was no fault of hers that there was only one child), who always messed up things and made her job more difficult. Because they were inconsiderate, she often wondered whether they loved her anymore and whether they were being deliberately nasty. She neglected to tell you that she had been too tired to make love with her husband for years, and that he, being a good man, had not gone running around, but had discovered the warmth of the barley. Rarely did anyone come to visit; some even interpreted Mrs. McGuire's efforts to wash their glass before they had finished drinking to be a signal to leave. Others were so uncomfortable that they would rather have been anywhere else, and there were others who refused to be bored out of their minds. But her house was clean. Her husband was drinking; her son was always out of the house; she was unhappy and soon would be worn to a frazzle. But her house was clean, always clean. Unless you looked real carefully. I hope no one buys her a magnifying glass.

The most that people can ask of themselves or another is that they attempt to do what is reasonable in normal circumstances and that they are willing to exert themselves in emergencies.

Perfectionism does not necessarily lead to pernicious self-directed anger. Some people seem quite able to blame everyone but themselves for their lack of success. But, on the whole, perfectionism and self-rebuke go hand in hand.

In the same way that unreasonably high expectations of oneself are learned, guilt is undoubtedly learned. Children who are punished whenever they express anger or any semblance of aggression soon learn to take their frustrations out on themselves, whether they are indeed culpable or not. The more children are punished for directly expressing anger, especially if the punishment is withdrawal of love, the more likely they are to injure themselves, to punish themselves whenever they become angry.

## Learning Self-Incrimination

A mother and her ten-year-old son went into a toy store. "Buy anything you want," she said. He looked around for a while. It was difficult, for he seemed attached to his mother's hand, so that he had to drag her wherever he went. Finally, he pointed to a toy bow and arrow. "That?" he asked. "Do you want to put out someone's eye?" she replied. That left no doubt that anyone who wanted a bow and arrow was some kind of monster. They settled on an erector set, without a motor, since you could electrocute someone with motors.

This child, barring intervention, is quite likely to acquire the habit of guilt, if the interaction just described between his mother and him is a fair sample of the way they characteristically behave toward each other. If every act which he undertakes which may have some aggressive intent is punished in a way guaranteed to reinforce the notion that he has an "evil nature," he is likely to learn both to punish himself for feeling anger, and to believe that he is an evil person because he feels angry.

While the example just offered depicts a boy and his mother in our culture, it is women who are more likely to be self-punitive. This has much to do with the way we define femininity. In our culture, the view is that women ought to be meek. They ought to be mild. They are certainly not to be aggressive. Women are to be submissive. They are to suffer without complaint. They are supposed to view their destiny as though it must be part and parcel of that of their husband. "Whither thou goest . . ." is a declaration of love, not individuality. Women are taught to be objects; they are taught to want to be chosen. If they are not chosen, say by their twenty-fifth birthday, give or take a few years, they are taught that it is because they are in some way defective. Of course, many women see through the social fictions imposed upon them, but, of those who do, how many will be able with clear conscience to declare that they are still women if they chose other than the well marked paths? No wonder depression is more common in women than in men.

Perhaps it would be well to summarize at this point. Depression and its symptoms spring from the interaction of a relatively small number of factors. One of them is the experience of loss; another is the tendency to turn anger inward against the self; a third is a heightened sense of responsibility. Perfectionism and a passive attitude toward the achievement of life's goals also make their contributions to the syndrome of depression.

# CHAPTER FIVE

# The Stresses of Everyday Life

If anxiety is produced when what we hold important is threatened, and depression is our natural and normal response to the experience of our loss, then clearly, in our trek through life, all of us must meet with anxiety and despair. The longer our lives, the longer and deeper is our experience with those antagonists. We are born and, thus, lose the tranquility of the womb. We grow into young adulthood and we must forfeit the pleasures of childhood for the increased responsibilities of the adult. We enter middle age, and we lose the vitality of our younger years and face the discomforts of physical decay. We become aged and we must prepare to give up that most precious of possessions, life itself. This inexorable fate we share with all living kind. It is not just that I meet destiny, but all those whom I love and who in return love me meet it, too. We must leave those who love us. Those who love us must leave us. At least in this life.

As if the unalterable wrenches of being human did not provide us room enough for grief, our society presents us with challenges which must be mastered if we are not to find ourselves plunged into the deepest despair. Erik Erikson termed these challenges "developmental crises."

A development crisis is a culturally programmed turning point in the life of an individual. These crises mark transition points in our developmental history. To successfully meet the challenges posed by these crises, the individual must change his normal way of behaving. He must make and accept radical changes in his style of life, changes for which he may not have been adequately prepared. If he is unable to make the appropriate adjustments, he may experience great pain and hinder his further development. Erikson identified eight such crises. There are undoubtedly more. The first of these he labeled *"Trust versus Mistrust."*

The crisis of trust versus mistrust occurs in the first year of life. It begins when the infant is thrust out of his mother's womb and into what must be a much more chancy and problematic existence. The infant's needs were once met automatically. After birth, whether the infant lives or not is dependent upon, among other things, the good will and expertise of the mothering one. Can the mother be counted upon? Can the infant, besieged by the force of his internal needs and stimulated almost beyond endurance by his environment, survive? Can the mother keep the infant's frustration within reasonable limits and convince the infant, so to speak, that though she or he has come into a strange land, there is some safe haven, someone in whom to trust? Can the infant be made to believe that, while the world is hard, it may be made tolerable by love, care and concern? Will the infant's groping, crying and thrashing be accepted, or will the infant be treated as a noisy, disgusting, malicious creature, more fit to be isolated than to be cuddled? The infant may learn to trust the world, to trust the mother, to trust his own needs, or the infant may be taught that life is precarious, that succor is unpredictable, that nothing is to be taken for granted, that no one is to be trusted. This decision, whether to trust or not, is not, of course, a consequence of a logical and conscious weighing of the facts by the infant, but an unconscious attitude stamped in by the force of his experience, an attitude which will influence all of his dealings with the world.

If the infant directs all of his energy toward survival, he may have little left over with which to cope with the next developmental crisis of childhood, that of *"Autonomy versus Shame and Doubt."* For, in the second year of life, the infant must adapt, in our culture, to another set of demands. The infant, once permitted the luxury of being fed, the luxury of relieving his bowel and bladder whenever he wished, must now learn to begin to fend for himself and to act in a way that is acceptable to his caretakers. He must learn to control himself.

Learning to control himself is likely to be an especially difficult task for the child who has achieved little success in having his basic needs met. He is not likely to understand that the new demands made of him provide him with the opportunity for further growth. Rather he is apt to be anxious about losing the little that he has, that which he has attained at such a high cost. His unwillingness and inability to achieve the standards of performance demanded by his parents, his reluctance to throw off his infant ways, ensure that he will be subjected to much humiliation, both at his own hands and at those of his parents. As a consequence of his failure, of his slowness, of his humiliation, he may come to view himself as defective, a belief which may cause him grief for some time to come.

The child whose attempts at independence are punished by his caretakers, who themselves prefer a docile infant to a growing child is also likely to develop deep-seated feelings of inadequacy and doubt, especially in the company of other children who are more adequate. Likewise the child from whom parents demand too much control too soon treads a rocky path. Such a child is doomed to experience failure. When he achieves success, it is always too little and too late. All of these children have difficulties in meeting the challenges posed by the crisis of autonomy versus doubt and shame, all of these children are marked by their failure.

The infant who meets the challenges of this period successfully either because of some inner strengths, the helpfulness of his parents, or both of these factors acting in concert, will have developed a sense of success, a feeling that he has some control over his own destiny. He will also be ready to meet the next hurdles that have been placed along his developmental path.

Before detailing the crisis of *"Initiative versus Guilt,"* a pause to bring into finer focus the concept of life crisis seems in order. Instead of seeing these crises as concrete, actual occurrences, for example, at two years of age, this happens and that happens producing this consequence, it is far wiser to view these life crises as metaphorical descriptions, abstract paintings, which attempt to capture with broad strokes the ebb and flow of life. Instead of viewing the resolution of these crises as fixing for then and forevermore the form and nature of the personality, it is far better to understand these crises as setting in motion or producing trends in development which, while they are not unalterable, do organize the experience of the individual along certain dimensions. No one completely fails the problems of living posed by these developmental tasks, and no one is entirely successful in meeting them. Each of us in some proportion feels both shame and self-confidence as a consequence of passing through these trials.

When an individual's feelings of self-confidence outweigh those of shame, he can be said to have passed successfully through the crisis. When, on balance, his feelings of inadequacy outweigh those of success, he can be said to have failed to meet the challenges posed by that crisis. Those who fail are not doomed. It is more difficult for them to move on to the next task, more painful for them to continue. They are less constant in their attitude toward themselves, less sure of their place in the world, at least for a while. But little in this world is forever, little is immutable, and most of what has been done can be undone.

The years from three to six are active ones for most children. Their ability to move about, both inside the circle of the family and outside of it, increases markedly. Their skill with language improves, and they come to use words increasingly well to gain a better understanding of the world in which they live. They are not yet constrained by the regimen at school, and, being on loose rein, they often seem to be bouncing off the edges of the world, curious about everything, trying to be adults without adult responsibilities, but remaining small and often contrary children all the while. Because of their high level of activity and their newly found ability to explore the world outside of the family on their own, because of their enhanced ability to communicate with others and gain information about the world, often information that is difficult to deal with, "What is dying? What is God? Why are people bad? Where do babies come from?," because their imaginations can leap beyond that which is comfortable for them, because they begin to socialize with other children, and come to recognize the difference between boys and girls, because of these things those years are exciting ones for both the child and his family. If the explorations are punished excessively at this time, children may come to overly inhibit their impluses, become fearful in their relationships with others, and in general adopt a rigid, safe posture. Too little limit-setting, too little discipline by their parents, on the other hand, may produce children who are unable to control their impulses and whose lack of control frightens even themselves, or fearsome children, whose behavior places them beyond the pale of civilized conduct.

Many abrupt changes occur in the life of the child when he goes to school. For the first time he is out of the home for a major part of the day. Mom or Dad are no longer a cry away. There are real standards of performance; you either learn to read or you do not. You are separated from old friends, you must make new friends. You must learn to sit still, learn not to be distracted, learn to play on cue at recess and not in class. For the first time you are judged by adults— not the parents who nurtured you, but by Miss Jones who runs the classroom. You are thrown into the education machine, raw material entering onto a conveyor belt from which there is no easy escape until each position in the assembly line is passed. No wonder that the next developmental crisis, called by Erikson *"Industry versus Inferiority"* is precipitated by the child's entrance into school.

This crisis is "failed" if the child emerges from his

early school experiences with the feeling that he is not up to snuff. It is failed if the child, fearful of failure, channels his energies into just conforming to the requirements set by others. This crisis is failed if the child devotes his life to pleasing others and in doing so fails to develop the joy in personal accomplishment or experience the pleasure of working for himself.

In our society, adolescence is a stormy time. Sexuality strikes many of us with the force of a tidal wave loosed by some evil sea god who takes his pleasure in maliciously complicating lives. Yesterday they were cute, respectable, well-disciplined, neuter children; today, dirty-minded, oppositional, disrespectful, dangerous beasts, possessing the bodies of adults and the judgment of infants. Adolescence is an in-between age. We know how to deal with children, we know how to deal with adults, but how do you deal with a man-child or woman-child? To make matters worse, though most adults have strong opinions about it, few feel comfortable thinking about sex, let alone living sexual lives, and adolescence marks the onset of the sexual awakening in their children.

While it is not considered modern to state openly that one believes that masturbation leads to mental illness, or hair on the palms of the hands, or poor eyesight, or what have you, many adults act as if they secretly believe it so, especially when they are judging others or admonishing the young. While it is modern to talk about sex and love going together to make for a perfect marriage, many adults live together without sex or love. What an impression our hypocrisy about sex must make upon the adolescent. What was your impression of how well your parents prepared you for sexual behavior?

No matter how important a role sexuality plays in adolescence, it is not the whole story. Adolescence, if it is anything, is a period of value crisis. It is a time when the adolescent must be able to learn to stand for himself, form his own opinions, and determine who he ought to be. Adolescence is often, therefore, a time of conflict between parent and child.

As with all socially programmed crises, it is difficult to blame the participants for what occurs. All are in some sense victims. It is not the parents' fault that our culture makes so much fuss over sex and regards the eruption of sexuality as marking the propitious time at which to demand vastly different social behavior from our offspring. Nor is it the fault of the child. But regardless of fault, new demands for adjustment are made upon both parent and child.

Erikson aptly labeled the crisis of adolescence "*Identity versus Identity Confusion.*" With that label, he wished to emphasize the core task of adolescence— identity formation. The job of the adolescent is to take into account the fact that he is no longer a child and to determine for himself the kind of adult that he wishes to become and the manner of life he would like to lead. To accomplish this, the adolescent must enter into a period of questioning and exploration. Before people can intelligently plan their future, they must come, at least in part, to understand where they are currently and why.

Not since their children were two and were screaming "No, No, NO" to every request are parents faced with such insubordination. No one needs to be told that a fourteen-year-old can get into more trouble than a two-year-old. Sometimes it seems as if the adolescent has written a horror movie and is auditioning his parents for the roles of blood-sucking monsters. Regardless of who is playing what, the acting and screenplay more often than not are horrible.

If it is the task of the adolescent to determine who he is, it is the task of his parents to guide and facilitate their child's self-discovery. If ever there was a more seemingly thankless task, few know of it. Dealing intelligently with teen-agers seems to be roughly comparable in difficulty to trying to put high button shoes on a wounded, angry water buffalo. But, if successful, the parents gain the long-run satisfaction of knowing that they have contributed greatly to the development of a real person, not just a very light carbon copy of themselves. Hopefully that is satisfaction enough.

Personal growth does not end when adolescence ends. Life's challenges never end. There is something more to learn, something new to do, another hurdle to leap, another pleasure to reap, or failure to experience, or loss to suffer. The crisis of *"Identity versus Identity*

*Confusion,"* if successfully met, prepares us to take on yet another major developmental task: coming to know others well. If the individual cannot learn to establish and experience closeness with others, sharing with others, be it in friendship or in love, he is open to the sadness, apathy, and loneliness of isolation. If the individual cannot merge his identity with that of others and, in doing so, transcend himself and his limitations and form with others, at least for a time, a new whole which surpasses by far each of its component parts, then he can never experience much of that which makes life meaningful. Whether one can learn to love and be loved determines whether one successfully passes through the crisis of *"Intimacy versus Isolation."*

As people grow older, they come to concern themselves not only with how well they are living, but for whom and for what they are living. They come to recognize that life is not spun out solely for their pleasure, but also to enable them to make a contribution to the lives of others. We have not been placed upon the earth merely to take and give what is there, but also so that we might create new meaning for others. It is not enough to say "I have done little harm." To be satisfied with our efforts, we must be able to declare, "I have left a heritage for others to follow." Not all of us can be Einstein and reshape man's understanding of the universe for generations to come. Not all of us can be saints and affect moral thought for centuries. In fact, few of us would be interested in making the self-sacrifice that such achievement would demand even if the ability to do so were within our grasp. But it is within the reach of all to contribute to man's future. Many of us will have children and have had through them the consolation that our lives will continue though we die. The love, concern, and good counsel we lavish upon our offspring will ensure a better tomorrow for all future generations. True, the world is hard and best intentions often go amiss, but if enough of us live well and teach well, though here and there one of our children is lost, on the whole, each of us will contribute to a better tomorrow. Having and loving children, of course, is not the only way to give new life to the world. Many cannot have children. What is required is that each of us attempts to make a positive contribution to the ages, be it by giving life to a new generation, helping that generation grow, or working to make the world a better place to live for those who come after us. We must choose for generativity and not for stagnation.

"Remember, the longer you live, the sooner you bloody well die," goes the Irish folk song. Each of us must die, and each of us must prepare to do so. If one believes in an afterlife, our whole life can be thought of as preparation for death. Those who live well will be well prepared to die, those who live poorly will not. Though many of us will be called before our three score and ten, an increasing number will not. Those of us who enter into old age must in some way face Erikson's crisis of "Integrity versus Despair." If we live as we ought, the last years of our lives may present us with the capstone of our existence. If we do not, the last years of our lives may bring us to despair and degradation. Old age is a time for summing up.

Old age is a time for wisdom. It is a time for sharing a living history. It is a time when we must recognize our humanity. It is a time of reconciliation and acceptance. It is time for humility and pride. It is a time for living well. It should be a time of integrity, not of despair, not the time for reliving lost hopes or dashed dreams, vain hates or imperfect revenge. Old age is not the time to feel that you are a burden; it is the time to reap what you had sown in good faith in earlier years. The crisis of old age must be faced bravely by the aged. The aged must be helped to be strong by those who are younger.

Unfortunately, our society does not often serve the old well or justly. It conspires against them. Instead of recognizing their accomplishments, we all too often consign the aged to the pit. We do not provide them with their wants, little as they are. We try to push them out, push them away. Anything to hide them from us, to prevent them from reminding us of our own destiny. We guarantee that all but the strongest of the aged, all but the luckiest will die in despair.

And, in so doing, we ensure too that our own ends will not be pleasant, nor dignified, let alone clean and pretty.

Trust versus mistrust, autonomy versus shame and doubt, initiative versus guilt, industry versus inferiority, identity versus indentity confusion, intimacy versus isolation, generativity versus stagnation, and integrity versus despair are crises which mirror the eight ages of man. They mark the path of his growth and development. They are milestones in the journey from total dependence in infancy, to productive adulthood, to wisdom in age. They mark points in the transition from a reflexive animal to a human being who has created meaning for himself and for others. They are turning points in our development as men. Each represents a challenge to a past pattern of behavior; each requires a sacrifice of the old. We must outgrow that which has served us well, for the sake of the new. Each crisis demands that we accept our loss. We must bravely meet our anxiety inherent in facing the unknown. We must attempt to fashion out of the future a place for us. They are turning points which dispose us to further growth or to developmental arrest. If we choose growth, no matter how painful these crises seem, in the long run we shall gain. If we do not choose growth, we open our hearts to fear and despair.

In addition to the programmed physiological and social crises that bring us pain in our daily lives, each of us falls prey to situations which may provoke anxiety and depression. Some of these are of our own making, some are not; all must be weathered. To list such individual crises would be difficult. Each of us creates and is vulnerable to different specific life stresses. Each of us reacts differently to the same events. But certain principles do hold. They have been mentioned frequently throughout this book. We become anxious whenever we are at risk, whenever we are threatened. We become depressed whenever we lose something of value.

It is far from easy to live well in this world. We are surrounded by much that will bring us down. Nothing is sure today. Nothing can be relied upon. Little is sacred. We live in a time of change, a transition time. When there is change, there is turmoil. Little has a "rightness" about it. Fewer and fewer aims appear to be truly legitimate. Where there is turmoil, there is threat. Our very way of life is threatened; our values are threatened. Our relationship to one another is threatened. Our relationship to God is threatened. When one is threatened, one becomes anxious. When one loses that which he values, he becomes despondent.

Perhaps societies, too, face developmental crises. Perhaps, there will be a new day. There is some comfort in that. But we must live *today* to have a more worthwhile tomorrow. How can one live well in an age of threat and despair? How, then, can one cope with anxiety and depression?

# CHAPTER SIX

# Coping

## *Developing a Comfortable Lifestyle*

No one has yet created a stress-free environment, but an imaginative person can do much to put emphasis on that which leads toward growth and to de-emphasize the stressful aspects of his or her environment. It is not an accident that prison riots tend to occur in summer in overcrowded facilities which do not have air-conditioning. Likewise, it is no accident that kindergarten teachers arrange their rooms into doll corners, an area for nature study, a free play area, and an area where children are expected to sit and listen. Most mothers and fathers have had a good deal of experience in engineering behavior through changing the "settings" for behavior. Most formal gatherings occur in the living room; good friends sit together in the family room or kitchen. Dad builds a fire in the fireplace and transforms a dreary day into a wienie roast. Mom feels tense and tired so she asks her good friend to take the kids for an hour while she takes a hot bath, regains her "cool" in privacy, and prepares a special dessert for dinner. We do all of these things and many more without giving a second thought. How much more might be accomplished with a little ingenuity and planning?

Every once in a while one ought to take stock of his daily environment. Does it express the kind of person you want to be? Does it facilitate hobbies, conversation, relaxation, play, study, family unity, contemplation, exercise, or friendliness? Or does it suggest rigidity, conflict, silence, and coldness? It does not necessarily take an interior decorator and a million dollars to reorganize your surroundings in a healthy way. Rather, it takes a set of goals, courage, and a little time. In some nursing homes, for example, "day rooms" consist of a centrally located T.V. and straight little rows of chairs. The people who come into these rooms do what is expected: they sit and watch T. V. and pay little attention to each other. If a person were withdrawn and shy to begin with, such an environment does little to encourage social activity on his part. Rearranging the chairs into conversational groups, introducing one or two game tables, setting up a modest snack area, and removing the T. V. and a few chairs to a corner radically changes the purpose of the room. People do behave differently, more sociably, in such settings.

Does your home express your life goals or does it fight them? Is it so far from your place of work that the gas station attendant knows you better than your children do? Is your living room a hollow showcase into which your children venture in fear and dread that they will bring some dust or disturb some secret symmetric order? Could it be put to better use? A home which expresses the individuality, the hobbies, the un-self-conscious hopes of a family has an atmosphere conducive to growth that $60,000 and a fancy address could never buy.

Psychologists have done some studies of "behavior settings." Certain findings emerge, again and again. The person who needs to be needed ought to place himself in a small community, be it a small rural town or a well-defined neighborhood within a large city. There is more pressure on a person in a small community to use all the talents he has. In a small high school, for example, the boy who doesn't make the basketball team may be asked to run the popcorn concession at the games. In smaller establishments and communities, there are more roles to be filled than there are people to fill them. "Big shots" are thrown into communication with "little shots," because they need each other; cliques are less prevalent, drop-out and turn-over rates are not as high. Superficial amenities such as politeness are observed since people are pretty sure they will see each other again. If you need to be needed, it might be worth the expense to find work in and move to such a community. After all, people have moved to Arizona for their asthma; why not move to Idaho for your integrity?

Conversely, bigness fosters competition, a degree of aloofness, excitement, and variety. For the confident, original, talented individual or the intrigued spectator who does not demand success of himself, there is always New York, Chicago, London, Tokyo and Los Angeles. In large settings, there usually are more people than there are roles for them to fill. Failure is a more common experience. Sometimes, it is possible to combine the assets of large and small settings, to find a community within a complex, a small compatible group of friends within a gigantic university, or a haven in a storm. One of the virtues of the "family" has been that it can fulfill this latter function. In its finer forms, it can give one a pleasant sense of being needed, even when the rest of the world seems rejecting and cold.

Needless to say, the family does not always facilitate security and growth. Instead, it might be a tight little knot of conflict and discord, something that is endured "for the sake of the children." Or it might be such a loose combination of people who happen to live in the same house that it no longer has the power to bestow warmth and trust. But the power of the family is such that it behooves a person to expend the effort to see that his family pulls together as a family should. The incidence of suicide is less among the married; married people tend to live longer than unmarried people; the incidence of juvenile delinquency is higher among children from broken homes. The statistics go on and on.

The conclusion seems to be "blessed be the tie that binds" one person to another.

Supposedly, to listen to the media, the family is on the way out in the United States. The family they talk about is the small nuclear unit of mother, father and children. The "family" has existed throughout history and throughout the world in a far greater variety of forms than most of us have considered. Its purpose has always been to educate children for adulthood in their particular society. Perhaps, the American family is in the process of changing its structure because it no longer does the job of educating as well as it should, and the demands of adult society have changed. Could the American family in its present form have become too insular and isolating? Maybe the "generation gap" is partly a result of children growing up without intimately knowing their grandparents, grandaunts, and granduncles. Maybe the inexperience and uncertainty of new parents is partially a fault of their never having had a hand in raising little brothers and sisters, cousins, nieces, nephews, and small neighbors. Lack of industry in adulthood may be the result of never having felt your labor made a difference to your family in your youth. One must decide what values your family wants to encourage and reorganize the setting and structure of your family to incorporate these values into daily life. People do not necessarily need to be biologically related to accomplish these goals in unity. A parent's best friends are often surrogate aunts and uncles to children. A friendly older woman is often a "grandmother" to a whole neighborhood. Rather than resent "intrusions" of others into the taut emotional life of your family, it might be well to look upon your family as a vehicle for broad social education and try to strike an appropriate balance between privacy and sociability.

Developing a healthy lifestyle requires more than congenial surroundings. Most of us could rattle off a stereotype of a well-rounded, emotionally healthy life: a strong network of friends, love, hobbies, exercise, work, activities, and spiritual depth. Likewise, most of us can recognize when someone is "playing" at this type of role, when their actions and their utterances don't ring true, or seem too good to be true. There seem to be traits within the people we admire and respect that set them off from those who are "going through the motions." Honesty, self-knowledge, a highly refined sense of responsibility, openness, empathy, appropriate expression of emotion, tolerance, balance, humor, a willingness to both give and take in life, integrity and a sense of purpose are such traits. Sometimes, we take a list such as this for granted, but the people who live these ideals do not; they work at it.

*Honesty.* The individual who is honest must recognize unpleasant things about himself and others. He tries to build his life on facts, not wishes. A woman needing advice may say about her friends, "I'll ask Mary. From her I will get a straight answer. I don't always like what she has to say, but with her I know where I stand. I won't ask Alice. She's always trying to figure out what I *want* her to say. This is too important for that sort of nonsense." Honesty also implies motivation to seek truth, to be dissatisfied with innuendoes, gossip, and mere implications. It implies the ability to know when to be quiet and wait. Honesty may be painful and must be tempered with judgment. Does the doctor tell the eight-year-old he will die of leukemia? Does he withhold this information from the parents? When he tells the parents, he does not leave them standing there, shattered. He follows through on his commitment to them.

*Self-Knowledge.*   Ever since Socrates said, "Know thyself," the importance of this attribute has been recognized. The person who knows his weaknesses will not enter upon contracts he cannot fulfill. The person who knows his strengths will utilize them. Take a very common example, the woman who knows she has a premenstrual depression complete with irritability and low resistance to illness. She does not ignore it or wish it away; she recognizes it and takes appropriate precautions. She does not plan a birthday party for 10 boys, ages 2 to 6, during this time. She couldn't take it. She takes account of her short temper and takes the kids to the park and tells herself "take it easy, take it easy" when her fuse burns short. She's not afraid to apologize. The people around her appreciate this.

*Responsibility.*   There is almost nothing more annoying to a parent than to walk into a room from which a loud crash has been emitted and be met with a chorus, "I didn't do it." The reflexive reply usually is "I don't care *who* did it. Somebody clean it up." The adult counterpart of these children is the buckpasser, an individual who fails to take appropriate actions for his mistakes. He, therefore, does not profit by them, does not alleviate the effects of them, and fails to do anything to relieve the guilt which his errors may thrust upon him. A responsible individual, on the other hand, carries many burdens, but guilt is only a tiny parcel to him. He is too busy carrying out his commitments and following through to stop for the luxury of self-pity. He is not afraid to say, "I did it," and reap either the attendant praise or punishment. He can incorporate his mistakes and learn from them.

*Openness.* This is simply the capacity to realize that yours is not the only valid, existing worldview, and that, maybe, you could learn something from someone else's worldview. For the open individual, the world does not end at the tip of his nose.

*Empathy.* Along with openness, empathy signals the ability to "walk a mile in the other guy's shoes," to try to experience the world as others might. In therapy, one might try to develop empathy by asking the client to role play, to act out the feelings of other individuals. The empathetic individual responds to others more appropriately, and with more understanding. Consequently, he gets less "flack" in return.

*Appropriate Expression of Emotions.* This is an art. Emotions should be highly refined, well-developed signals for thought and action. They should not be an occasion for becoming frozen, for exploding, or for frightening yourself. An adult should be able to pound his fist on the table and alert all and any that he feels their actions are wrong, that there are some things he will not allow. An adult should be able to get mad at himself for his errors and allow the anger to motivate him for appropriate action. He should be able to love and to hate and to keep these emotions under control. The only known way of developing the appropriate expression of emotions is practice! Learn to get constructively mad when you're mad. Learn to recognize when you are overreacting with giant emotions to an insignificant incident. Don't bottle your feelings up; become an artist in expressing them.

*Tolerance, Balance and Humor.* The person with these attributes is able to put his life and his actions into perspective. He does not believe his way is the only way. He strives to understand his place and function in the scheme of things. He learns not to take himself too seriously. His perspective is broad; he is not focused unnaturally on himself, in this place, at this time. He looks at the Milky Way, ponders infinity, and laughs about his troubles at the office.

*Reciprocity.* This is the ability to accept graciously and give wholeheartedly, and to feel bound by your promises, spoken or unspoken.

*Integrity.* So far, the whole chapter has been about integrity. A style of life which summarizes and expresses the values of an individual, which encompasses his conflicts, strengths, and weaknesses, is a statement of the wholeness and integrity of the individual.

*A Sense of Purpose.* Here, no one can help. It is known that great and creative people have it. There are no formulas for finding it, except "look around, there's plenty to do." The people who do have a sense of purpose are carried outside of themselves by it. They orient their lives to goals, challenges and rewards which transcend their psychological, physical, and temporal boundaries.

In finding a comfortable, individual style of life, it is important to experiment, to try out something new and to cast away those things which do not fit. Models and ideas abound in history, in books, and in life. Life is too short to live falsely, to live in conflict or to live in despair.

## Coping With Anxiety

No matter how well he lives, a person, by dint of being human, cannot live without becoming all too familiar with the experience of anxiety. No one is perfect and this is an imperfect world. Though each of us has had extensive practice in dealing with anxiety, there are undoubtedly times in each of our lives when our usual techniques for keeping anxiety in check are not totally successful. At such times, it is wise to re-think the typical, habitual methods we use to deal with anxiety in the hope that we might find more effective substitutes for them.

There are good ways and bad ways in which to cope with anxiety. Hiding is usually a bad way. There is an old folk tale that seems applicable. A man learns that Death is waiting for him. To escape his fate, he flees to another city. He is met at the gates of that city by a hooded man. The hooded man greets him. The hooded man tells him, "I was becoming worried. Your name was given to me. I was to meet you here today to take you with me; however, I learned that you were in another city. I was concerned that you might not arrive for our appointment. But, I am relieved that you have come. Come! We must go." The hooded man was Death. It is often as difficult to flee from our anxieties as it was for the victim of the folk tale to flee from Death. No matter where we go, anxiety, just like the personified Death, may await us. For we often carry anxiety with us, and there are few places in which we may hide from ourselves.

Any technique we employ to deal with anxieties that does not remove their cause will often prove to be futile and will frequently be in itself harmful. No matter how comfortable alcohol, for example, may help us to feel, drinking is an exceedingly poor method by which to cope with our fears. When the bottle is empty, our concerns remain. Likewise, when the third or the fifth bottle is empty, our concern will remain. It may even be increased by the use of that which has alleviated it temporarily. But there is little utility in detailing the myriad ineffective ways in which we attempt to control our anxieties. The purpose of this book is to suggest ways that work, techniques that reduce the wear and tear of life.

How to deal with anxiety? The way to begin to cope with anxiety is to recognize that it has a "normal and useful" function no matter how debilitating an emotion it can be if it gets out of hand. The "normal" function of anxiety is to give warning, to warn the individual that danger is at hand. The first step in dealing with anxiety, then, is to come to understand that it serves to warn us. Anxiety warns us of a potential threat to our well-being. Warnings are not to be ignored, nor are they to be feared. They are to be accepted, respected, and acted upon.

Having been warned, having been put on alert, so to speak, our next task is to identify the threat and its nature. If we can take that step, it is much to the good. It may not always be possible to do so for a number of reasons, good and not so good. For example, we may have taught ourselves to avoid thinking about danger and have succeeded to the point that we fail to recognize danger when it is upon us. We may wish so much to believe that our husband is faithful that we ignore even the lipstick on the collar and the late hours spent at "work." If we cannot recognize the threat, a circumstance that we shall cover later on, our situation is more difficult, though not hopeless. But let us assume, for the moment, that we can identify the source of our fear. What to do?

What one is able to do about anxiety depends a great deal upon the nature of the individual, the unique circumstances surrounding him, and the nature of the threat he faces. In spite of this, however, the same broad strategy applies in diverse situations. The individual must take steps either to reduce the threat or reduce the consequences of the threat to himself or to others he values.

Marge Smith is a very shy, thirty-six-year-old, unmarried legal secretary. She works very hard for her boss, so hard, in fact, that she often spends her evenings and Saturdays typing reports for him. He really ought to have hired another secretary; but she was so willing to do the work of two and he wanted to avoid the added expense and the break-in period that would follow if he hired another woman that he let it ride. She knew his marriage was on the rocks, and though he did not know it, she loved him. Undoubtedly much of her seeming dedication to the job was in reality an attempt to impress him, but regardless of the motivation behind her endless hours at work, she had no time left over in which to socialize with others. She was his girl Friday, Saturday, Sunday, and Monday, and on through the days of the week.

Well, his marriage did break up. It was a messy affair. He had three children, two girls and a boy. They suffered the most. Yes, there was another woman. It was not Marge. While Marge was holding down the office, he was out holding hands. Marge felt as if she had been kicked in the head. She had always been a somewhat anxious person, but now she was constantly on edge. She could not concentrate. Luckily her boss was so busy with his own problems that he did not notice. The climax came on her birthday. She was at her parents' home, sitting down to dinner, when, for no discernible reason, she panicked. Later, her parents told her she was very upset and had fainted. When she came to, she took a bit of time to pull herself together, and, feeling somewhat better, she decided to go back home. The next day, at the insistence of her parents, she made an appointment with a social worker.

Together, the social worker and Marge managed to piece together what had happened. In simplified form, what they had discovered went something like this. Marge was in love with her boss. She had come to hope that she might marry him, a fantasy to be sure, but Marge lived most of her life through fantasy. In fact, Marge had channeled all of her hopes toward that fantasy. She was a shy person who found it difficult to meet other people, and if she was going to marry her boss, there was no reason to go out of her way to meet others. Why go through the pain of dating others when her future was assured? To make matters worse, her parents put her under considerable pressure: "Stop being an old maid. You're not growing any younger, you know. Soon you'll be too old to catch anything worthwhile." When her boss remarried, her hopes and plans were dashed. In a flash, she became a thirty-six-year-old woman with no prospects, a sterile, middle-aged, old maid who had produced no grandchildren for her parents. She felt doomed. She did not know how to begin again. She experienced a great deal of anxiety.

Therapy was not simple, but it was successful. Marge was able to understand that her boss's marriage did not necessarily signal the end of her life. The threat was not so severe as she had thought. As soon as she came to see that she had been kidding herself about marrying the boss, the fact of his remarriage became less threatening. As soon as she realized that she could learn to meet others without becoming unduly upset, and that others enjoyed meeting her, she became less anxious. As soon as she came to understand that she could lead a meaningful life without being married, and if she so chose, there was still enough time in which to find a mate, her tension diminished.

In sum, Marge became less anxious when she discovered an effective way in which to reduce the threat posed to her by the remarriage of her boss.

Another example may prove useful to illustrate our point:

Bruce Thompson was a junior majoring in sociology at the state university. He knew that if he was going to make a career in sociology he would have to go to graduate school. To go to graduate school, he would have to score well on the Graduate Record Exams (GRE) in addition to obtaining good grades in college and securing three positive letters of recommendation from his professors. He was not worried about his grades, or the letters, but the GRE scared him. He often "choked up" in important exams and this was, if nothing else, an important exam.

The examination was scheduled for late September; here it was June. He was worried already. "If I become more upset," he thought to himself, "even if I know the material, I'll blow it." With disaster facing him, Bruce, being an intelligent fellow, took the following steps to deal with his feelings. First, he obtained all the information that he could about the test. One of the folders he received contained a number of sample items and told where he could get more. He ordered those, and with them began to practice for the exam. While he might not know the specific items that were going to be asked, he could become quite familiar with their format. Soon, he found himself thinking the right way, and as a result he found himself becoming more confident.

Next, he worked on time-pressure. He usually did well when he had time to think, but typically he became upset when someone stood by his shoulder with a stop watch. So he had a friend time his practice sessions. He was not happy with having to work so fast but he became accustomed to it.

He thought about taking a speed-reading course, but decided against it. He felt that he could read quickly enough to do the job. Likewise, he dismissed the idea of trying to review all of the work he could be tested upon. That was just too large a task, and quite unnecessary; he was a good student. If he tried to relearn everything, he reasoned, he would just add to his troubles. Instead, he decided to reassure himself about his competence in a relatively small but quite important area—statistics.

While he was practicing to answer the kind of questions that would be posed, practicing taking timed tests, and reviewing statistics, Bruce also took the time to think a great deal about the actual circumstances he would face on testing day. He imagined going into the building, entering the test room, and sitting down.

He imagined receiving the test materials, hearing the instructions being read to him, reading them himself, and starting to work on the test, calmly. The first few times he rehearsed in his mind's eye the sequence of events he was nervous. He soon became more comfortable with his mind's play.

In addition to preparing for the exam in the ways

**105**

just described, Bruce also took steps to minimize the influence that this one exam could have on his life. He realized that if he wished, he could take it over. That reassured him. He explored alternatives to sociology as a career. He reviewed his aims and the path he had chosen to attain them. He decided that there was, at least for him, more than one way to skin a cat.

By the time the day of the test had arrived, Bruce had things well in hand. He was still more than usually nervous, but he was nowhere near a state of panic. In fact, if anything, his level of alertness was well suited to the requirements of the task before him. He was "up" enough to work more carefully and quickly than was usual, but he was not so "high" as to carelessly rush through the exams, skipping items he was afraid to tackle.

How is it possible to reduce a threat to manageable proportions? There are many ways to do so. Most of us hit upon some of the ways that often prove useful.

It is usually best to begin by assessing your situation with a cold and critical eye. Granted this may be difficult to do, and it may require that you ask for help, but it is necessary nonetheless. You must be objective; you must seek to view your difficulties from afar, as if you were helping someone else instead of yourself. You must ask, among other questions, "What do I stand to lose?" I am afraid of something. That something poses a threat to the way things are or the way I would have things be. What is that threat? What of importance to me is at stake? Sometimes the answers to those questions will come easily. Other times the answers will be obscure. Sometimes you will have to cut through your complicated situation, divide the forces that you face at one level, before you proceed to the next. Human lives can be extraordinarily tricky and complicated. When they are, if we are to understand them, they must be simplified, at least for the sake of analysis.

Coping with anxiety usually becomes easier when the source of stress has been identified adequately. Such identification may make it possible to avoid the stress. This is often a wise course of action when the threat seems irresistibly strong or the harm that may be done is considerable. It would be folly for an alcoholic to go to a bar and to demonstrate that he does not have to drink, better for him to avoid coming in contact with alcohol altogether. But some threats cannot be avoided. These must be faced squarely. That does not mean, however, that they must be faced stupidly. Bruce, in the preceding example, determined that to get to graduate school, he would have to take the GRE. His plan of action was intelligent. He prepared himself to tackle both the exam and his fears about it. He also planned two escape routes for himself if he failed the test: he could either take the test over, or prepare for a different career.

Sometimes, however, knowing what one fears is not

enough. On occasion, each of us may find himself in a position from which we feel there is no escape. We feel trapped. We feel the walls closing in on us. Everywhere we turn we face disaster. At such times it is best to seek help, to seek out those who have had experience dealing with such seemingly impossible difficulties, to seek out those with no axe of their own to grind, and who have had experience in guiding people out of difficult places. Go get help. It is both foolish and immoral to suffer when there is no need to.

Just as people may find themselves immersed in what appear to be impossible situations, they also may become quite anxious without being able to identify the origin of their discomfort. To cite one example, relatively few people who are phobic can recall being frightened by the object of their terrors. There are more people in Chicago who are phobic about snakes than there are snakes in Chicago. And, it was not by accident that anxiety was originally differentiated from fear on the basis of whether there was or was not an identified threat. If there was an identifiable threat, the person was said to be fearful. If there was not, he was considered to be anxious. That you might not be able to identify the source of your anxiety is, therefore, not unusual. It should not add to your discomfort. It should not cause you to despair, nor does it mean there is no hope for you. Rather, it means that the techniques available to you with which to reduce your discomfort are more limited than would be the case otherwise. Because of this, if your nervousness comes to interfere too much with the way you wish to live, it may become more necessary for you than for others to seek professional help. But more of that in the next chapter.

## Coping With Depression

As you might expect from reading the discussion of depression presented in a preceding chapter, coping with depression is often a difficult, though not impossible, task. Successful treatment of depression requires that the individual makes good his loss in some way and orders his life in such a way as to ensure he attains a reasonable level of security and stability for himself in the future.

In practice, almost all individuals survive the loss which precipitates their depression. Depression tends to be a self-limiting condition. Most people recover a semblance of their usual level of functioning after a time. However, many of those who do "get better" fail to make the alterations in their style of life which are necessary to reduce the likelihood of their getting caught up in depression again. More than a few of these people will behave in such a way that will almos guarantee that they will suffer from further episodes of depression. How may one avoid those pitfalls?

Let us presume that you are feeling low. You have just lost someone or something that has been of considerable importance to you. Perhaps a loved one has died; perhaps you have broken an engagement, or your daughter or son may have gone off to college; or you feel you have acted against your sense of morality and as a result you feel lost. Any number of events which might have brought you down have occurred and struck you with a vengeance. The normal reaction to such a loss is depression. Undoubtedly you will become depressed, too. Accept the depression. While it may be useful to put on a false face for others, try not to kid yourself. You have lost something quite important; it is only reasonable that you mourn the loss. Relax, you are not superman, you have a right to get upset, as well as an obligation to yourself to do so. Pick a safe place, then emote. A good friend can really help at this point. Confide in that friend about how you really feel. Do not be embarrassed. One of the things that friends are supposed to do is help.

Remember, when people are depressed they are not normal. Depressed people are slower; they are not as vivacious, they make more mistakes than usual. Do not make the mistake of getting down on yourself over those things for which you have little responsibility. You would not punish a sick man for running a fever, would you?

Depressed people are usually angry people. They frequently ask the question "Why did this happen to me?" Even if there is no good reason to do so, most blame themselves for their sorrow. This undoubtedly

happens for a number of reasons. For one, very few
people live without guilt. The natural assumption of
the guilty is that, whatever the evil deed was, it has
finally caught up with them, and they and all they
love, are being swept up in some manifestation of cos-
mic justice. The grandiosity of the guilty has few
bounds. For another, most of us do contribute in some
measure to our difficulties. We say the wrong word
at the right time, or the right word at the wrong time.
Sometimes we are stupid; sometimes we are negligent;
all humans are. It is both right and proper to experience an appropriate amount of guilt and anger at
ourselves for our misdeeds, both of commission and
omission. But, the purpose of such anger and such guilt
ought not to be the mutilation of the soul. That is immoral as well as self-indulgent. Instead all that is expected of us is that we undo the harm that has been
done, if that is possible, and that we take steps to avoid
a repetition of our bad behavior in the future.

Accept the fact that it is natural to be angry at yourself when you are depressed. Accept the fact that
depressed people are angry people. Work off that
anger in physical activity. Swimming, riding, bowling,
and walking are all excellent ways to do so. But do not
accept the debilitating guilt that often accompanies
depression. Call yourself names if you must, but do
not believe completely in the merit of your self-accusa-
tions. If you do find yourself unable to adopt a reasonable attitude about your sins, secure the opinion of

**111**

another about them. Choose an objective, honest, knowledgeable person who can give you an honest answer. Listen to that answer. Too many times people go out of their way to obtain only opinions with which they agree. Far too often, people only listen to what they want to hear. Depressives usually want to hear about how they have been wronged, how they have sinned. Depressives are usually biased themselves. This bias must be taken into account by the depressive himself and by others with whom he may deal.

One thing you can be sure of is that it takes a while to get through a depressive episode. People just do not rebound quickly from a severe loss. It takes time to put your life in order, to start things up again. As with many things, "slow but steady" does the trick. If you are depressed, give yourself a chance. Remember that just as exhaustion often accompanies the flu, it often accompanies depression. When you are exhausted, it takes a bit of time to recover, but recover you do. Do not rush yourself and then become disappointed with your lack of progress. All that would accomplish would be to add insult to injury.

Once you feel that you have brought your depression under control, you may have to face the difficult prospect that depressive episodes may reoccur. Times and places of special significance have the power to evoke sorrows anew. For example, if you have lost a loved one, the anniversary of his death, his birthday, holidays you once shared, and places where you once walked together may open old wounds. Time may mellow the effect. Accept the fact that you will be more vulnerable at certain times and in certain places.

Before he can feel "whole" again, the person who is depressed must in some way recover or replace what he has lost. If he has lost love, he must find love. If he has forfeited his self-respect, he must in some way recapture it. Such requests are made quite difficult by the inability and unwillingness of the depressive to engage in life again. No one finds love in front of the television set or sitting alone in a half-darkened room. No one regains his self-respect by shunning the company of others. No one recaptures his self-esteem while staring at the bottle of whiskey he has just finished. No one recovers lost friendships while rocking in a chair with the stereo turned up to "blast." Somehow the person who is depressed must be brought back into the stream of life. Slowly, he must get his feet wet again. Slowly, perhaps, but surely.

Clearly, reintegrating someone who is depressed into the normal pattern of everyday living is difficult. The depressed person must decide to begin life again; he must come to the conclusion his life must go on, in spite of the pain it may bring him. He must agree to allow himself to be vulnerable. He must reason that the game is worth the risk. Many people who have suffered personal loss come to that decision almost automatically. Others must be coaxed or cajoled by themselves or others into choosing life. They must lead themselves or be led by others, no matter how difficult or onerous such a task is, along those paths which once brought them pleasure. Did they once enjoy going to the movies? Try the movies again. Perhaps by the third show, perhaps the tenth show, some of the old pleasure may return. Did they love good food? So all food tastes flat now, try again tomorrow and tomorrow; perhaps they will forget themselves and enjoy the meal.

Especially to be favored are those activities which, by their nature, involve the depressed individual with congenial company, for the person who is depressed must re-establish his ties to others. Cards? Great! A church committee? Great! Coffee klatching? Marvelous! As the person comes to participate in group activities more and more, his responsiveness to the group should also increase. In this way, the depressive comes into sustained contact with others who may help him to satisfy his own needs and who, in their own right, may bring him pleasure. In this way, he is led into the network of mutual obligation that characterizes normal social interchange. When you make appointments with others, you must behave in a different fashion than you would if you were the sole custodian of your time. You must pay attention to keying your activities to the tick of the clock. You must dress appropriately. You must talk to and do things with others. In these ways, the individual's re-entry into the stream of life can be engineered. Once he is among the living again, once he has made the decision to live, it may become for him possible to recapture that which he has lost, or to find someone or something of equal or of greater value in its place.

Learning to cope with depression is undoubtedly important. Learning to live the type of life that will enable you to minimize your vulnerability to depression is of even greater importance. Prevention is almost always cheaper than cure, especially if the price is reckoned in human misery. Even if you have a shy and passive disposition, it is easier in the long run to enter into close relationships with others when you are feeling well than when you must carry the additional burden of depression.

To protect yourself against severe depressions, you must learn to live well. You must learn to take pleasure in living. You must learn to go out of your way to cultivate an intelligent and moderate style of life. You must take an active role in determining your own destiny. You must not passively place your life in the hands of fate or others more than is necessary. Remember, few people know you as well as you do, and few people, if they must choose, will place your interest ahead of their own. Learn, no matter how difficult it may be, not to take your errors too seriously. Keep in mind that you are but human, and being human means that, no matter how much you may try, you will still make mistakes. It is far better to learn from those errors than to punish yourself for them. Let us not belabor these points. A word to the wise ought to be sufficient.

# CHAPTER SEVEN

# Help: When to Get it, Where to Get it, and What to Expect

## When to Seek Help

Why do people go to the doctor or the dentist? The answers are usually quite simple. They go because it's time for their check-up, because they are in pain, or because normal functioning has altered very noticeably or alarmingly. A young mother usually receives a list of things to look for from her pediatrician so that she will know when her baby needs medical attention. Evidence of pain, swelling, high fever, continuous vomiting, diarrhea, a drastic change in activity level or appetite are enough to send her to the telephone for assurance that everything's all right or assurance that the doctor will diagnose and treat her baby's illness. At first she may tend to call him about every little thing. After she has gained experience, she may develop keen judgment about her child's health. Busy as they are, most pediatricians will agree that it is better to call too often than too seldom. Doctors also have the advantages of seeing their patients for regular check-ups and having access to disease *prevention* techniques.

The clinical psychologist, on the other hand, usually meets his clients when they are in acute psychic pain or when a situation has grown to such gigantic proportions that no one could possibly overlook it. He often sees the aggressive child only after school authorities have told the parents that the child disrupts classroom activities or has injured other children. He may see a disturbed adult only after a series of anxiety attacks have occurred or the individual's usual functioning, measured by such things as job performance or school grades, has been impaired. In the area of prevention, he faces the enormous problems of developing and teaching better child-rearing practices, helping to reduce the amount of stress present in entire social systems, and researching, researching, researching to find out about the nature of man and man's interactions with other men and his environment.

Psychology, psychiatry and social work are relatively young disciplines. There is no thermometer which measures whether or not you are hot under the collar. There is no pail to collect psychological vomit and give material evidence of self-disgust. There is no needle which will immunize a person against failure, self-doubt, or worry.

When *should* a person seek psychological help for anxiety or depression? It is easier to answer the question: When *do* people seek psychological help for anxiety and depression? They seek it either when they cannot cope, when they are in mental pain, or when those around them can no longer stand it—"it" being the person's behavior, demeanor, or mood.

For children, parents must decide the proper time for help and the appropriate source of help. School adjustment is a major factor in this decision. Child clinics commonly have an increase in the number of children they see every October after school begins and a decline every summer after school lets out. Academic problems and social adjustment problems in school act as a major signal to parents that something is wrong. The good student who begins to fail subjects, the child who continually refuses to go to school when he enjoyed school before, are sending out signals that something is wrong. The understanding parent realizes that children often are not able to put complicated, perhaps even socially unacceptable thoughts into words, and may go to great lengths in their behavior to "tell" the parent that something is wrong. The formerly active child who, after the death of a favorite aunt, refuses to leave the yard, even after an appropriate period of grieving, is signaling his parent. The slightly aggressive child, anxious about losing control of his aggressive impulses, who starts bragging about how many friends of his are in juvenile detention homes, should be coming through loud and clear. He's asking for help: "Don't let it happen to me." The child whose behavior radically and inappropriately changes is often trying to communicate something to his parents. Child clinic referrals sometimes increase after holidays. Parents may overlook a lot of things, but a kid who stamps on his Christmas stocking and mutters "Ah" as he turns dejectedly away from his new bike probably could find no better context in which to contrast his present misery with his former joy.

We all have short-term adjustment problems in which a good cry or a good friend is all that we need; kids do, too. When the unusual behavior persists or becomes desperate, then help is needed. The four-year-old who starts wetting his bed shortly after the new baby comes home is not uncommon. The four-year-old who wets his bed for months, who starts defecating in his pants, who becomes withdrawn and uncommunicative is crying loudly for help.

In summary, when each day becomes a new zone in a battle with your child, when hopes for a peace treaty have dissolved, when his behavior, sleeping, or eating patterns have changed, it's time for outside help.

For the adult, the decision to seek professional aid poses a different set of problems. To some individuals, seeking help is the same as an admission of weakness. "I should be able to solve this myself." If a person's central problem involves his self-esteem and he reacts to it by glossing over his faults, making excuses, becoming rigid, in short, by being defensive, it may take nothing less than a bulldozer to get him in a door marked "psychologist" or "psychiatrist." If you happen to be this person's husband or wife, you are placed in an awful situation. You can wait until he has a severe anxiety attack and becomes frightened; you can wait until the weight of depression settles like a boulder on his back and talk him into seeing a physician about his fatigue; you can threaten, cajole, deliver ultimatums—tell him it's him or you; or you can go for help yourself to learn ways to cope with the stress your spouse is placing on the whole family. Many times people are afraid to tell others that they seem to require professional help. "If I told him that, he'd walk out on me. He thinks people who go to psychiatrists are babies who can't take care of themselves." So tell him anyway; he may react differently than you thought. If he does walk out it's just one indication of his shaky adjustment, and at least you tried. If there is a priest or physician he respects, the idea that he needs help may come from them with better results. Many rabbis, clergymen, and priests have taken courses or degrees in counseling, social work or psychology and may give therapy in their own right.

No matter what, see that you and your family get regular physical check-ups from a good doctor, preferably one who knows you pretty well. What may appear to be a psychological depression may be hepatitis or a thyroid dysfunction or any number of illnesses. Conversely, a low grade infection which drains your energy may put you at a disadvantage when you must cope with stressful situations, and may even precipitate what is commonly known as a "nervous breakdown." A person can only cope with so many problems at one time: an overburdening of his body and mind may cause reactions throughout his whole being. It is well known, for example, that after prolonged anxiety, one's resistance to illness diminishes.

When *should* you seek help for anxiety or depression? When your symptoms are no longer mild and temporary. When the situation you blamed for your problems has long since passed by and your misery remains. When you feel you cannot manage. When you cannot get through your regular activities. When you cannot sleep, eat, love or play. Or when you are facing more than any normal person can bear and need help to get you through a crisis.

## *Where to Get Help*

There are nearly as many types of therapies as there are therapists. Certain groups of professionals can easily be distinguished, but within these groups practices, philosophies, and personalities vary widely. Professionals differ in their training, their approach and the type of problem to which they prefer to address themselves. The problem of choosing a therapist is further complicated by the fact that states differ greatly in their licensing requirements for mental health professionals. Some states insist that psychologists and social workers pass a lengthy series of examinations constructed by outstanding members of their profession before being allowed to practice in the state. Other states have *no* requirements. Literally any yo-yo can hang out a shingle proclaiming "guidance and counsel" and do his best—or his worst. It is a good idea, then, to have a list of therapists recommended to you by someone whose judgment is trustworthy: your physician, your school principal or psychologist, your priest or rabbi, your community board of mental health. At this point, you might check the therapist's experience and background through local professional organizations, e.g., the state psychological association, the state psychiatric association, and examine the diplomas on the therapist's wall. Finally, you must make a personal decision that you trust the therapist.

*Professional Training and Therapy.* To become a psychiatrist, an individual must complete medical school, his medical internship and his residency. In addition, he receives three years of training in the psychiatric unit of a hospital or at a mental institution. After two more years of practice in the psychiatric field, he is examined on his knowledge of diagnosis, his knowledge of the structure and functions of the brain and nervous system and for his knowledge of various psychiatric therapies. If he passes the examination, he is awarded a certificate which makes him a Diplomate of the American Board of Psychiatry. The important

**123**

thing to remember is that psychiatrists are M.D.s and are the only mental health professionals who may legally prescribe medicines or drugs. Beyond this, psychiatry encompasses a broad range of treatments. Some psychiatrists undergo psychoanalysis themselves and practice the "talking cure," psychoanalysis based on the principles of internal conflict, unconscious motivation and development of defenses outlined by Sigmund Freud and his successors. A few specialize in narcotherapy, a type of drug therapy in which the patient is stimulated to bring up forgotten incidents by drugs. Most practice a combination of the many therapeutic techniques available to them. Their training often emphasizes the interrelatedness of physical, mental, and emotional functioning. If one's anxiety or depression were closely allied with physical factors, e.g., depression sometimes occurs in conjunction with hormonal changes during "change in life," the psychiatrist would be a recommended therapist.

The clinical psychologist has a different background. He earns a Ph.D. degree, not an M.D. degree. It takes about 7 years of graduate work to complete training for a Ph.D. in clinical psychology. The curriculum usually includes courses in psychological testing, psychopathology, personality theory, statistics, experimental design, and electives in perception, cognitive functioning, sociology, and anthropology, etc. The Ph.D. candidate must complete extensive original research for his dissertation and also have at least one year of supervised therapy experience. After he completes his Ph.D., the clinical psychologist, counseling psychologist or school psychologist may apply for a diploma from the American Board of Professional Psychology.

The requirements include three years of supervised therapy experience and enough additional experience to total at least four years of postdoctoral experience. He must be a member of the American or Canadian Psychological Association. Then he is examined for his professional competence in therapeutic techniques, his knowledge of research and theory and his judgment about ethical matters. The committee questions him about a transcript of an actual therapy record. If he passes the examinations, he becomes a Diplomate of the American Board of Professional Psychology.

Psychology is a very broad field. For example, it is possible today for an educational psychologist to get a Ph.D. in "Reading," and specialize in the diagnosis and treatment of reading disorders, a source of anxiety for many school children and their parents. Psychologists may be testing experts (e.g., the "IQ"), vocational guidance counselors, as well as psychotherapists. The range of therapeutic techniques available to them is quite wide. Behavior modification, the scientific manipulation of behavior through the administration or withholding of rewards, is a technique useful in combatting phobias and behavior problems. Relaxation therapy, in which the anxious client is taught to release the tension from major muscle groups, is an offshoot of behavior modification. Hypnosis, psychoanalysis, and crisis intervention, in which the therapist gives support to the client and helps him to alter a threatening environment, are all examples of the therapeutic procedures used by psychologists. Carl Rogers, a psychologist, developed client-centered therapy. He believes that clients will be able to solve their own problems if the therapist fosters an environment of warmth, genuineness, and unconditional acceptance of the client, his thoughts, and feelings. In psychology as in psychiatry, there are almost as many ways of helping others as there are helpers. If a summary could be made, one might say that psychologists are interested in helping clients learn new methods, more effective methods, of dealing with problems, and in finding ways to make the client's psychological environment more livable.

Social workers constitute a third major group of mental health professionals. In working for their master or doctoral degrees, they might take courses in community organization and planning, sociologic processes, anthropology, abnormal and social psychology, statistics, economics, government, medical information, social casework, social research, public welfare, social insurance, and economic and social legislation. The social worker interested in doing psychotherapy might take courses in psychosocial development, psychopathology, psychodynamics and principles of clinical psychiatry in addition to working under supervision for a year in a family agency, guidance clinic, or psychiatric unit of a hospital. Traditionally, the social worker has placed emphasis on the family as a social unit and has worked to alleviate economic or social stresses by working with community resources and government agencies. Today, many social workers have opened private offices as psychotherapists and have incorporated such techniques as psychoanalysis or behavior modification into their practices.

Often the psychiatrist, psychologist, and social worker work together in clinics and hospitals, each lending his particular expertise in helping a client. A psychologist may refer his client to a psychiatrist to see if tranquilizers would be recommended. A psychiatrist may ask a social worker to find methods of alleviating the economic distress of one of his patients. The social worker might ask the psychologist to test his client to help find out why "Johnny is a slow learner." And all of these professionals might help train "lay therapists" in the community (nurses, teachers, ministers, recreation directors, camp counselors) so that they might use therapeutic techniques when mild emotional problems arise.

Happily, more and more insurance programs include benefits for psychotherapy so that the individual who needs help need not become anxious and depressed about the bill. In a country in which half of the hospital beds are occupied by the "mentally ill," psychological help is not a foolish luxury. Sometimes it is a necessity.

## What To Expect

Miracles: Not quite. An easy formula for effective living: Well, not really. Good advice: Consult Ann Landers for that. Help: Yes,if you have a good therapist and stick with him.

Much research has been done on what happens during therapy and what the outcome might be. Most of the research concerns the "talking" therapies, psychoanalysis or client-centered therapy. A few findings stand out consistently. Most often people expect that therapy will be guidance; someone will tell them what to do. Instead, they find out that for most therapies, it is participation. They work hard during that therapeutic hour. In the beginning, clients may ask the therapist in frustration, "What do you want from me? I've spilled my guts to you; what do I do now?" If a client leaves therapy at this early stage, often it is because his problems were too minor to motivate him for further therapy, or because it proposed too real a threat to a very rigid defense system. At this stage, as the client works toward the source of his problems, the therapist may caution that things will get worse before they get better. The client's motivation for therapy may go down and he may wonder why he's spending his time in this office. Clients often report feeling weighed down by responsibility, feeling very alone, at this point. Something has to give.

The client finds he both desires and fears change. He is not happy the way he is; he doesn't know what he is going to become. He may be acting out with his therapist some of the feelings he had about his parents, his marriage partner or other important figures in his life. This tendency to treat the therapist as if he possessed characteristics similar to those of important people in a client's life is called "transference." Through recognition of the transference, the therapist hopes to help his client understand his habitual ways of relating to other people.

Next, the client discovers some of the thoughts and feelings he had denied or pushed out of consciousness. "Why, I really am an angry person," a client may exclaim. He finds out things he doesn't like, but must admit that they are part of him. This requires a reorganization of the client's personality, a somewhat rocky process. Take the case of a person, call her Jane, who repressed feelings of anger, because in her childhood, every time she became angry, her parents became very cool toward her. "You naughty, ungrateful child, to speak to your mother that way. Get out of my sight," Mom would say. In her adulthood, every time she began to get angry, she would feel anxious because she felt others, like her mother, would turn away from her. She felt depressed, because even as an adult she was naughty and unworthy. Through therapy, she re-discovers her anger, still a child's anger, because it hasn't been refined and tempered through years of practice at being angry. Her husband complains "Since you've been seeing that stupid psychologist, you've been behaving like a baby." Her son says "Mommy, don't yell at me. I don't like you anymore." Her family was used to dealing with her the way she was before; when she gave them liver twice a week when she was mad, when she didn't express her anger directly. If she sticks through this, the therapist teaches her, helps her realize new ways to express her anger. The denied feelings become a part of her personality. Often before this process is quite complete, the client will experience a very black time. "It is darkest before the dawn." Then follows the release from misery. For Jane, the process might go like this:

"Last Wednesday, I felt so tense all day, everything bothered me. I could hardly look at John. Everything he said annoyed me. Finally, I exploded. I must have yelled at him for a solid hour. I told him he was inconsiderate, he was a rotten father. He didn't appreciate me. I even told him that as far as I was concerned he could take a few lessons on how to behave in bed. Then I got so scared. I thought he was going to leave or hit me. But he didn't. I was shaking. We just looked at each other for a while. Then, I don't know how to describe it, life went on. The world didn't come to an end. About two days later it hit me what happened. I felt terrible about what I said to him, then I thought, well, a lot of it was true. And then, I don't know, I felt so free, so relieved. We went out to dinner this weekend and it was, well, it was perfect. I joked about things I never joked about before. Even John said he was glad to see I wasn't taking myself so seriously anymore."

The client may come for a few more visits as he or she vacillates between feeling relieved and sure of himself and uncertain about his ability to handle new stresses. Then, therapy is over. It may be a lengthy process or a relatively short one depending on the client's problems.

Of course, individualized "talking" therapies are not the only therapies. The client may choose group therapy, in which a group of individuals with similar problems, under the guidance of a therapist, assume a therapeutic role toward each other. The client, whose problem is tied to an identifiable situation such as loss of a loved one, may choose a therapist who will give him support and reassurance. A client may prefer a direct approach and go to a therapist who will tell him what to do. Most therapists, by the time they become established, have had quite a bit of experience. They will tailor their techniques to fit the individual and his particular set of difficulties.

Anxiety and depression, so much a part of everyone's life, need not overshadow the very process of living and growing.